# "Imagineer"
## "the fine art of deciding where to go from here"

*"Skim it for some immediate, applicable insights. Or follow the author's lifelong journey in an easy-to-read style. No matter which approach you take to Imagineer Your Future, there's value in what's inside."*

**– Peter Reese**
*Branding Consultant and Author*

*"Les amazes me by not only his inventions, but his creative talent for grabbing people's attention. His commitment to making the world a better place is awe inspiring and now I am blessed to call him friend. Les, thank you for sharing your entrepreneurial wisdom with me and anyone fortunate enough to read your book or meet you."*

**– Tonja Waring**
*MyPillow Infomercial Hostess
Founder, The Manifesting Mindset
Best Selling Author,
"The Power of Manifesting"*

*"I have a thriving seven figure business in tech education today partly because of advice that Les LaMotte gave me "work on your business instead of working in it". Les's advice helped me build a business with financial and time freedom."*

**– James DeCicco,**
*Author/Speaker
MasterTheGigEconomy.com*

## In Humble Thanks

*"My life has certainly been surrounded by oceans of fantastic people. My spouse, my children, my family, friends, business partners, and those willing to help in times of life's greatest storms and celebrate in life's greatest victories. Most important of all, of these relationships is my daily walk with my Lord Jesus Christ."*

*(– Les LaMotte • Imagineer, 2019)*

*My hope is that this book inspires you to fully grasp your gifts and core passions and use them to inspire the world around you.*

**Imagineering Your Future!**

Les LaMotte • Imagineer

Les LaMotte His College Sophomore Grandson (Middle)
Given to him in 2019 and his 2021 Graduate Grandson's
Portraits given to them for 2020 Christmas Gifts.

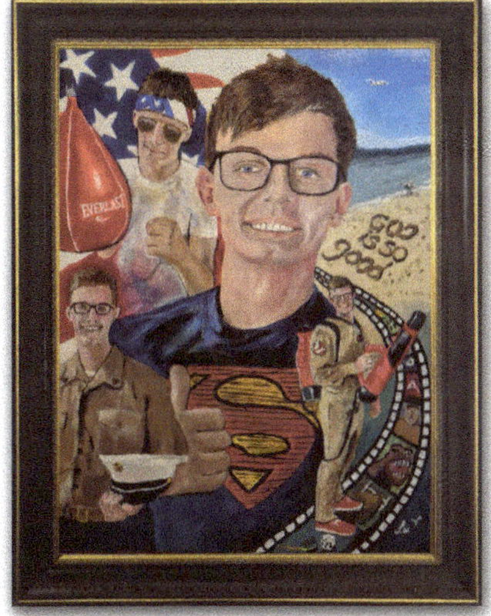

## Who is Les LaMotte, Imagineer?

*"My rock is my beautiful, and wonderfully talented spouse Vicky, of almost 50 years, we raised our family of three outstanding and gifted children to grown adults with their fantastic supportive spouses giving us twelve beautiful and amazing grandchildren."*

(– *Les LaMotte • Imagineer*)

### *"Les is an outstanding motivational speaker, author, designer and multi-award winning ASCAP / singer songwriter"*

Les possesses a charisma all his own. He is an expert generalist and leader in all that he accomplishes. He is a *"connector of people"* with the keen ability to quickly win friends by genuinely caring about them, motivating, and connecting them to others who can help them to succeed beyond their wildest dreams.

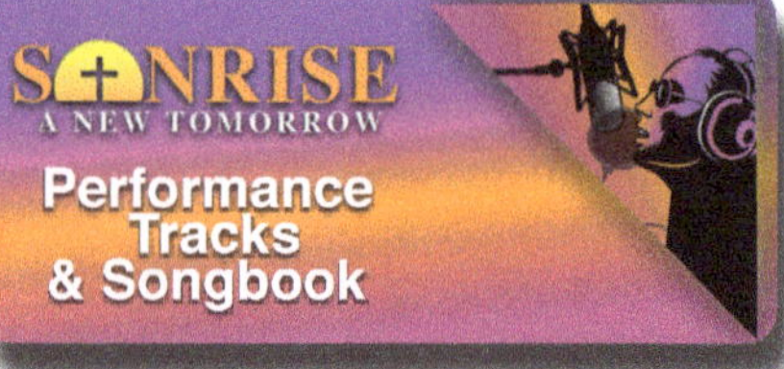


**Nine Multi Award Winning Original Song Album with Accompanying Songbook**

# Table Of Contents





*The Design and Organization of This Book*

*1. This book is divided into Concept Groups of Chapters by using Color Keyed side taps.*

*2. The Vertical Chapter Titles allow you to quickly thumb through the Concepts and Chapters.*

*3. This $ Symbol indicates that the Xcel sheet you may down loadable for FREE on my website: LesLaMotte.com*

*4. This "Imagineer" ™ symbol represents areas of specific learning opportunities.*

## Why Everything You've Ever Learned Is Important!

*In Memory of*
Lester "Les" Allen McPheron

*Happy Birthday*, Grandpa Les (June 14,1900–1970, Flag Day). Thank you for lending me your name, and I loved being in

Washington DC, June 14, 2005, on your birthday and thought of you while I stared up at Lincoln at his memorial. What an impressive place to be and celebrate Flag Day and your birthday together! I have kept the flag tie that I bought in Washington DC and hung it up in a case with this photo of President Lincoln to remind me that you were also born in Illinois.

I salute you and Grandma Irene for choosing my mother Katheryn McPheron *(LaMotte)* out of all the other children at the home in Sauk Center, Minnesota. Especially

taking her home to South St. Paul to love and accept her as your very own daughter.

Grandpa you always taught me to love and respect our nation's flag and took the time to show me how to fold it, care for it, hold it in high esteem, and run it up the flagpole you made in our front yard. You imparted to me the significance it held for you and why that was important to our corporate futures in the United States of Freedom and Liberty. How you never forgot how you gave of yourself in duty and sacrifice for our country, and that is why it was such a meaningful symbol to you. I could see in your eyes and your visceral body language as you spoke about it with the honor and dignity that is given to an old friend.

You explained to me in great detail the circumstances of being in the First World War in France. You shared your diary in which you capture the memories of your friends who met their end there, and you were sure to point out that their death was surely ones performed to keep us free. I captured the words, and it is now in the Military Library of Congress in memory of all US service personnel who served. Thank you for your great sacrifice for our country. You were an eyewitness to history in France at the Armistice Day, November 11, 1918, to the end of the war. Your deep, rich character was truly inspirational to all of our family. I loved your fantastic and dignified Hudson car. I felt like a king when riding with you in that black supercool car. Most of all, thanks for your great deep singing voice and that was so wonderfully stuffed with spiritual humility and reverent prayers at Thanksgiving and Christmas dinners. Little did you know you would inspire me to launch my career in music singing and songwriting. I would liked to have shown you the many awards I received for my music; I am sure you would be very proud of all my accomplishments. Most of all, thank you for teaching me to make kites from sweet pine, newspaper, string, and white glue. You gave me the inspiration to study architecture and the use of tension, which expanded my horizons as we sat and assembled kites together. Who would ever have guessed that it would lead



WWI Diary is available on Amazon. Authored by Les LaMotte for his Grandfather Les McPheron

to my 1997 invention of the Xtra Lite Displays® aluminum pole tension structure or that I would receive five US patents and many international ones from that simple lesson you took the time to share with me? That it sold around the world before it sold in the United States and ran unequaled for fourteen years? Your contribution to my life is priceless, Grandpa.

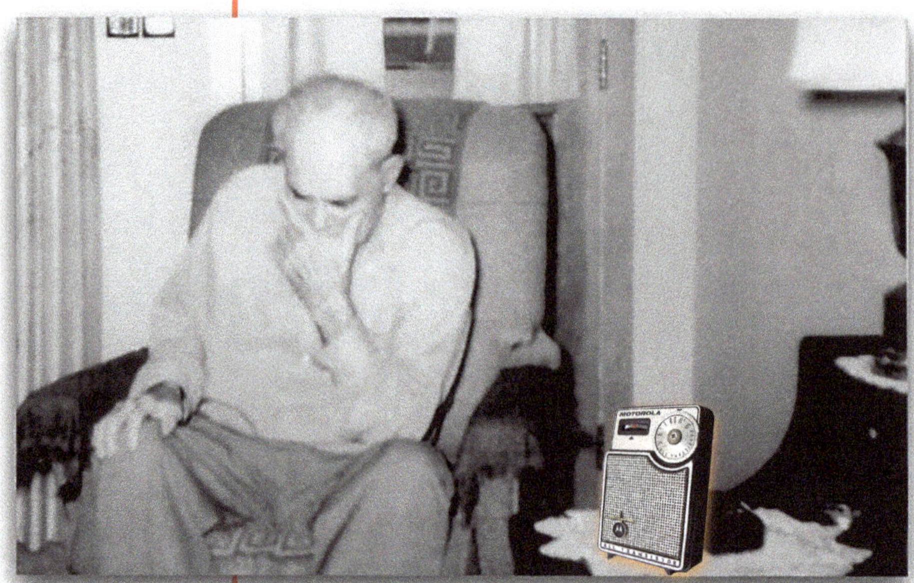

I cherish those thirteen years we became real pals as I looked after you when you became blind at the age of only sixty-five. Those many nights and afternoons sitting with you and Grandma with a glass of her favorite red wine, listening intently to the details of the latest NASA launch, the tragic death of John F. Kennedy, and so many other advances that you loved to talk about with me on the front lawn while you sunned your arthritic knees and we shared your beer together.

I will always picture you sitting in your chair in the living room of the "little house" that my father built one $2 \times 4$ at a time. You were constantly exploring the world, but unfortunately, you could only listen to it on your new miracle transistor radio. The hundreds of times you would call me over to fix the earphones and honing my knowledge and skills working with electricity and audio engineering. Little did you or I know that someday, I would be using much more sophisticated recording gear and it would advance to even using my cell phone to record and edit books to sell online at Amazon. Grandpa, you would have loved to have an iPhone—*it is so you.*

*"You modeled for me what it means to grow gardens of food, build places, and imagineer kites."*
(– *Les LaMotte • Imagineer, 2019*)

At the time I am writing this I am sixty-seven, and I am also challenged as you were with health issues. But thank God, modern medicine has helped save my eyesight up to this point. Grandpa Les, you modeled for me what it means to grow gardens of food, build places, and imagineer kites. You gave me such a rich and multifaceted fulfilling life. Planning and building things with you was a pleasure. Of course, I appreciated the small financial rewards as well along the way, which inspired

me to begin my own entrepreneurial ventures as a kid and for my future.
One of your biggest surprises in my life was when you and Dad gave me the Christmas gift of a used O scale Lionel train set with all the fun stuff anyone would want. Plenty to set up my eight-by-eight foot train table in our basement. It even had a cast-iron locomotive that made real smoke. That train set taught me so many lessons. One of the lessons was in our leaky basement. I quickly learned about electricity several times; it was a real shocking experience. One of the most

mind-expanding things you gave me at the young age of eight was the use of your fully equipped wood shop. You taught me how to use and maintain your large power tools, especially the table saw.

One of the saddest days of my life was while I was just getting settled into my sophomore year at Moorhead State University. I received a phone call from Mom and heard the news of your passing. Grandpa, I know that today you sit at your Savior's feet. I can't wait to come and see you soon. I love you, Grandpa, and you continue to be the greatest influence in my life and career as an Imagineer. You were the best!

*Thank you Grandpa Les!*

Your adoptive grandson,

Les LaMotte
*Imagineer*

*Grandma, Katheryn (LaMotte my mother),*
*and Grandpa Les McPheron*

## From this Pre-Design and Simple Photo That Cost $14

"Born out of the need for a lighter-weight display for the music industry. First introduced in São Paulo, Brazil, and used in a Mercedes-Benz showroom."

**Mercedes-Benz**

## To an international micro-business that produced $14 million in revenue in fourteen years, marketed in thirty-six countries worldwide!

The Octahedron-tetrahedron or better known as the Geodesic Dome... is completely composed of triangles.

These triangular structures are extremely light weight while supplying immense strength and support.

Les LaMotte, founder of Xtra Lite Display Systems, based his original XL1 patented design on the sound engineering principles of triangulation.

### Unique Patented Features
• Commitment to quality, engineering & detail

• Confidence in the performance of your investment

### Lightweight & Easy to Use
• Easy Set-up and Take Down

• Save Big $$$ on transportation costs

• Easy and more cost effective to store

• Take It Anywhere

### Systematized for Simplicity
• Intuitive Products - less training required

• Uniform, "Designer Look"

• Less Parts — easy to manage

• Simplifies Customization

• Invest at your pace

### Emphasis on Graphics
• Uninterrupted - virtually seamless Graphics!

• Greater impact on customers and potential customers

• Easy access and change-out

• Interchangable within product family

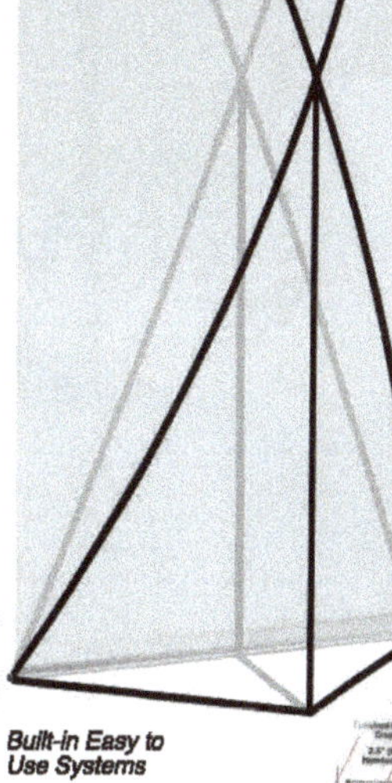

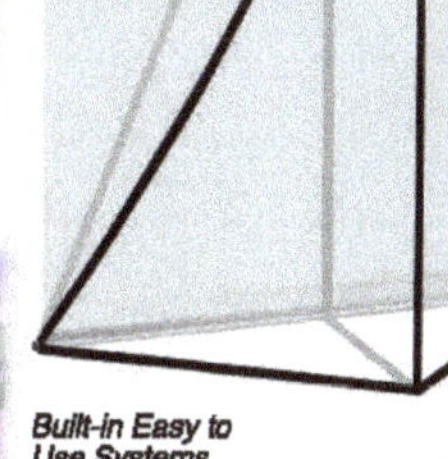

### Reliable Technologies
• Tension Engineering for crisp graphics

• Pole Pockets for easy graphic changes

• Easy Change sizing

### Uncompromised Aesthetics
• Unique appearance; Visually appealing

• Visual impact in selling / branding effort

• Focus customers on your brand image

## Where Does One Begin Writing Their Book?

Is it at the beginning of your life that you start, or is it your ultimate creation, or void of your spiritual walk, the people that have influenced you, only secular people of business or highly spiritual people who have challenged your vast thoughts and dreams? In my case, most of the things that I experienced I learned came from doing and doing it over until I got it right at least in my eyes. Yes, I attended the *"school of hard knocks"* or you might call me a *"bootstrapper."*

However, I also studied art and graphic design at Moorhead State University in Moorhead, Minnesota, right next to Fargo, North Dakota. You probably have heard of Fargo with the movies and all. And yes, they are pretty accurate depictions of the ultraconservative environment of Midwest lifestyle and mind-set back when I was attending college in the early '70s. It simply can't be only about my life, my music, my design experience, my spiritual awakenings, and family; it is a mixture of all of them that has made me who I am today. After all, to call yourself an Imagineer means you lead a complex life like

Les LaMotte and Peter Reese preparing for the GMA Show in Nashville, where it all started.

MacGyver, schooled in enlightenment and problem solving with many hundreds of ideas of the past, present, and future technology, all while living your life in various stages of your own growth, development, and experience.

No one time is any more valid or life changing than any other time. No business experience can be told without how it affected you personally. So the following story of my life and work experience are one and the same. You must comprehend my base beliefs, my motivations, and my influences from many angles to even begin to understand what it takes to become a true Imagineer. By reading through this book, you will begin to see that perhaps you have already made critical decisions allowing you to move forward in *Imagineering Your Future*, or you may have to peel back some layers of your life's onion to rebuild and strengthen the base structure to be able to support your journey to a new life of "*Imagineering Your Future!*"

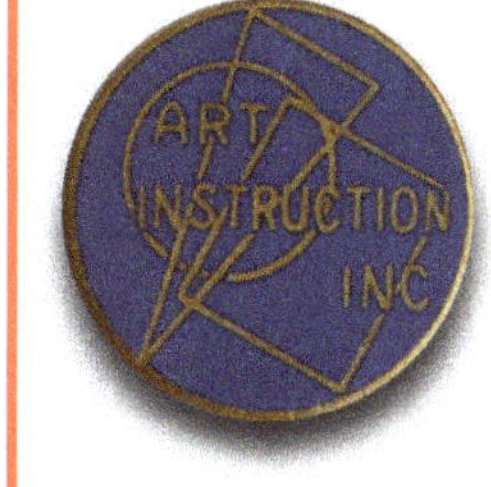

I am certainly not saying that everyone else who chose to go their own way or just struck out on their own path into hippie colonies and whether they learn it from someone else or in a classroom or from a social culture or "*the whole earth catalogue.*" This group just chose a different path from the narrower one that I chose or found because of the people who influenced me in my church and college in Fargo/Moorhead area. Very conservative and mostly Scandinavian, they lived in a Bible-centric lifestyle that I could understand and relate to.

A year before high school, I began taking art classes from *Art Instruction Schools* (who 50 years later became one of my clients with Xtra Lite Displays) whose headquarters were located here in Minneapolis. I studied very hard to learn all that I could about art and painting. I suppose art encompassed my life at that time. I may not have played hockey, football, and baseball as much as others, but that was okay, as that was their interests. When I entered high school, I already knew how to draw and paint. This is where I begin realizing that art was what I was called to do. Many, including my mother, always said that she could pick out my artwork in my grade school classrooms when she came to visit. She said that my art stood out to her as having a greater distinction more recognizable as art than many of the other students. It was these early encouragements by my mom and others that drew me to achieve my dream of becoming an artist and Imagineer. Okay, you got me, I really didn't know what an Imagineer was at the time, but as I paid great attention to it through TV shows

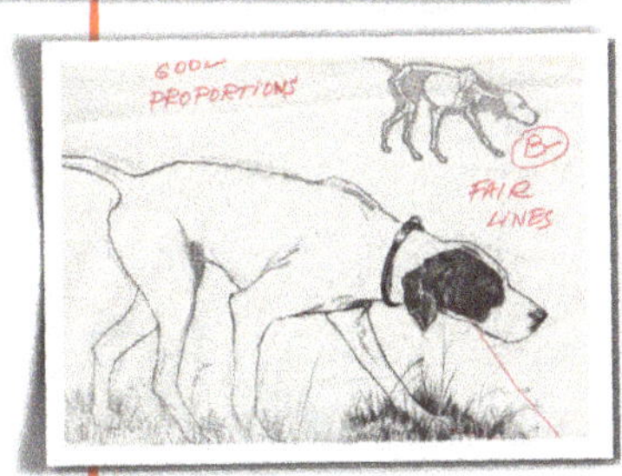

Les LaMotte started his Art training on January 2, 1965 in 9th grade by correspondence.

like Walt Disney, I began to gather information certainly much less expensive than the cost of sending men to the moon in those days.

## Early Influences in Imagineering My Future

In my early life after high school, looking at options for where you should go next was really not an option at all. Your hopes for the future were either constrained by your financial situation or planning on attending college or trade school—that was it, other than the armed forces, which we were hot and heavy into the Vietnam War at the time. If you joined up, you were given about two to three weeks at best, and life was pretty much over. There were no other options, and certainly nothing was ever spoken about finding one's passions and what did they have to do with anything anyhow! Nor could I even pick up a book on the subject let alone my smartphone, which was only a fantasy in comic books like Dick Tracy or something. I don't know, I never read any of those. However, I met one of the actors from the Dick Tracy movie as he was the husband of my mother's best friend.

The one who just goes out to follow their dreams and makes the best of it, well, there really wasn't much encouragement there either. Money was tight; you might say that ideas were also extremely tight as the modern design of the big-box stores, computers, and the next latest TV gadget was just not the norm or even thought of yet. This kind of upper class lifestyle was reserved only for the elite who could get the scholarships for Notre Dame, Harvard, or Yale. Otherwise, you would go to attend more affordable state colleges or travel out to California and live on the corner of Haight-Ashbury in San Francisco. At that time, most were inhaling strange-smelling weed or *"grew out your hair to make room for your brain"* coined by Larry Norman in one of his pithy tunes. Larry actually was one who lived in those neighborhoods. His songs of the changing power of Jesus Christ in the lives of people during these extremely

rough places and times of the late 60's and early 70's which was known as the *"Jesus Movement"*. Larry highly influenced me and my music after meeting him I spent sometime talking with him at Moorhead State University. His music and message was loud and clear as he tried to revive, update, and warn the Church in those perilous times. The general public was experiencing the protest of the Viet Nam War with loud and massive anti-war protests and violence. It was heavily entwined with the love gen and hippy cultural movement which today has morphed into the Antifa commonly considered to be part of the far-left. However, Larry's prophetic message rose above all of that and he gladly pointed his *"One Way"* finger high noting that God's love is what everyone is really looking for. Unfortunately the Church in general could not grasp the authentic need nor did they respond with the right attitude of Christ's love towards those who were then seekers. So the vast majority of the hippies moved on to almost everything else accept following the one true, God. Hence a general turning away from God and detachment of normal society begin to go adrift and the Church being conservative, did not respond soon enough or with the right actions and a large percent of our US and worldwide population pulled out of the God standard that was the sound principles and bases from which our country was so wonderfully founded on. Although Larry was not quite appreciated by everyone especially the Church at the time he eventually went on to become known as the *"Pioneer of Christian Rock'n Roll"*. He met his Lord and Savior Jesus Christ on February 24, 2008, after several years of wrestling with his health. Rest in the arms of Jesus, brother.

1

*"We need a solution we need salvation let's send some people to the moon and gather information . . . it only cost 13 billion . . . must be nice rocks."*

*(– Larry Norman, 1973, Only Visiting This Planet.)*

### If I Were Twenty-One Again . . .

A few years ago, I found a request on LinkedIn, and I responded with this story about what I would do if I were twenty-one again. Now wouldn't that be sweet? I would have just finished college and gotten married and moved to Madison, Wisconsin, for my first job with InterVarsity Christian Fellowship as the graphic designer and a member of the financial development team.

Well, if I could unlatch the gull-wing doors of my DeLorean time machine and go back in time when I was twenty-one, I would have to reel in about forty-five years consisting of graphic design, marketing, film, international product packaging and product design, entrepreneurship, family life, working in Africa, winning awards for my singing and songwriting, give back my five patents, give back my airline tickets to just about everywhere in the world I have traveled and all of my friends I have made around the world and right here in my neighborhood, my

Les and Vicky LaMotte with their
12 Grandchildren, Christmas 2020.

beautiful and supportive spouse, Vicky Larson LaMotte, and my three wonderful children, Joshua, Jordan, and Jody, their lovely wives and husband and my twelve beautiful and talented grandchildren that are the apple of my eye. Now that would be a tragedy!

The good news is I get to keep all of these memories, family, and relationships and now convey to you how you can start building on a solid exciting foundation for your life that is worth living by starting to *"Imagineer Your Future!"*.

Les LaMotte and his eldest son Lt. Colonel, Joshua J. LaMotte. This is Joshua's Core Purpose that he had written a few years earlier to establish certainly and focus to his life's purpose.

## Discovering and Empowering Your Core Passions!

### Let Your Graduation Hat Hit the Ground First!

The biggest mistake I have observed that young graduates make after throwing their hats into the air is not realizing it is not the end of high school, university, college, or tech school, it is the beginning of their life mostly unencumbered by their family and it's the time for them to dig deep down inside of themselves to identify what really motivates them to discover and pursue their true *Core Passions!*

My self, well, I simply failed this first test very badly, most likely, because I allowed others to take me down a road they thought was good for me. What I didn't realize is that once you start making cartwheel tracks in the fresh clay of your life, it will begin to mold your mind and your life, leaving you searching to get back out of the rut you keep traveling in. You know, if you ever lived where it snows when driving and trying desperately to steer your car on glazed ice, you want to go one way, but the ice under your tires is forcing you to do all kinds of other things that usually with a fast correction will quickly put you in the ditch up to your nose in snow. Now what?

## Career and Technical Education (CTE) Programs

*"Two-year technical degrees are a viable alternative to four-year universities, and prepare students to enter a modern 21st Century workforce. CTE programs allow students to get real-world experience in skilled trades that employers are looking for. Almost half of talent recruiters at Fortune 1000 companies report trouble finding qualified candidates with 2-year STEM degrees, and about 50 percent of all STEM jobs are open to workers with less than a bachelor's degree. There is a skills gap in America that CTE programs can help fill."*

*(Jason Lewis, member of US Congress, State of Minnesota, from constituency's newsletter, 8/2018)*

### Have You Been Listening?

So do I wish that someone would have told me these simple but profound truths at the tender age of twenty-one or sooner? The answer is *absolutely yes*, which is what I hope you are saying right now. I may have been told in hundreds of ways, by thousand of people, but, was I ready to listen? Well, that is a horse of a different color, as I remember it in The Wizard of Oz.

*"When the student is ready the teacher will appear."*

*(Origin unknown)*

## Don't Flunk Your Final Self-Exam

Self-examination is a lost concept in today's culture, as we are taught to follow the crowd and where they go and what they do is what is expected of us without really thinking about who you are and what you want, Yes, **YOU!**

I say **STOP!** I mean **STOP!** Yes, right now, **STOP Reading**. Do not go any further before you take the time to do a thorough self-assessment to discover your core passions.

### What are your 5 Top Core Passions®?

Write down what you think they are here…

1. _______________________________________________

2. _______________________________________________

3. _______________________________________________

4. _______________________________________________

5. _______________________________________________

Don't know what your top five core passions are or would you like to find out for sure? Take the ***Core Passion***® Assessment online like I did to find out:

**MyCareerSeeker.com/Imagineer/…** *One Time Fee: $90.00 USD*

Les LaMotte's Core Passions Assessment results in 2007.

## Remain a Lifetime Student

Unfortunately, when you are eighteen to twenty-one years old, you actually believe that you will *"live forever* and *know everything, so why do you need to listen to anyone!"* What could you possibly learn from someone who didn't even own an iPhone or smartphone when they were your age anyway? Everyone knows that young people are flexible and highly resistant as if they are as hard as steel and impossible to screw up. After all, you believe you have sixty years and nine lives to fix any major mistakes you may have stumbled across. If you believed that, then you would also have to believe perhaps that choosing your life directions can also be corrected over the next forty to eighty years. Yes, this is possibly true if you live long enough, but I am sorry to inform you that this may seem like a simple solution, but as life accumulates more and more weight and burden is applied, it is much like the truck at the auto show that as it moves forward, the weight is moved farther and farther back to the rear wheels, causing it be eventually stopped due to too much weight. The truth is that as the years add up, so does the weight of your life, bringing you to a place where you may reside in a *"stuck position"* and the result may possibly that just at the time we think we can make the changes that we should have in our youth, our old age no longer allows a full recovery. Potentially it can lead to a very unhappy lifestyle or work at a job and an environment much different than you had planned on and for a much longer time than you could ever imagine.

Okay, you're a new graduate with your whole life in front of you. You have just spent twenty-one years in preparation. However, you might be asked to live out someone else's life purposes with their expectations they have assigned to you even upon your birth. Yes, I am talking about your parents or those around you who highly influence you. Here is where you need to *"put the brakes on."* **STOP** and find your key core passions, and do not be jilted into going to college or finding a job or getting out of school to get rich or something extremely unrealistic for you. I know, you can't see it at this time very clearly because your mind has been

> ## *"If you have no critics you'll likely have no success."*
>
> *(Origin unknown)*

trained on taking orders or thinking that agreeing with others is expressing your love for them. Or maybe you are just trying to make their life comfortable by accepting their life choices for you. Reality is that you have stepped into a world flying at the speed of the internet, going every which direction and you're only hoping you're not being thrown under the bus in the process. So what do you do now? What are your options?

What are you really going to do to find true success as you dodge the bullets and missiles being thrown at you from every direction, potentially urging you to do or fulfill what others want you to do or to live through you? Really, is that what you want to do and how you want to live your life?

> *"Remember, it is YOUR LIFE, and only YOU are responsible to God for what you do with it and who you become."*
>
> (*– Les LaMotte • Imagineer, 2019*)

1973 Les LaMotte - Senior at Moorhead University, Moorhead Minnesota Pursuing a BA in Art & Emphasis in Graphic Design.

## Where Do You Start on Your Journey?

### Make No Plans

Okay, let's start with making *"no plans"* until you are fully out of school, period, **Full Stop!** No, it is not the time to get into a heavy relationships and possibly risk having to support a family or with the complications and extra expense of a child without being ready to commit to being married just because your hormones are racing. Or that you just thought that you should do what everyone else is doing or beginning unmarried relationships out of some half-baked concept of saving money by splitting the costs and justifying and trading your personal innocence for economic realities you haven't taken the time to figure out just yet. Or much worse, because that's what is expected of young people of your age group and justify it on the basis of its trending as the new norm for the majority.

Why settle for the common, the ordinary, as if there were no other alternatives by falling under the spell of the peer pressure of the majority anyway? I thought we are individuals with our own gifts, talents, and desires?

Why has this *"groupthink"* principle overtaken us so strongly today? Why would you want it to? The only true answer can be that you are not okay in your own skin! Why else would you choose that kind of weak thinking? Possibly, because you were convinced early in grade school that you had to work only in groups and lose yourself and take on a new identity of the group. Accepting a lower grade because messed-up Linda totally let your group down and so you all received an incomplete or low grades, did you think this was right too? Of course not!

Les and UN Representative observing the new Chinese roads built just south of the oil fields in 2010 Malakal, Capital of the Upper Nile of South Sudan.

Then you move on to senior high school and you again fell under the groupthink by believing that the only way to have friends were those whom you knew at that time and you were without a choice to find and make others. I can tell you from my personal experience that those I hung around with in high school I have hardly seen once or twice throughout the last fifty years of my life maybe at a reunion or something. Why is that? I believe it is because the friends you make in college or after high school actually become your real best friends. After all, the heavy pressure to find your identity under the influences of the cliques, bullies, and crowd pressure of finding your pecking order in school and that entire childish process just goes away quickly. Leaving you left with who you really are and the difference of what you have become. Isn't right now really the time to do your homework on **YOU** to find out who you really are?

What if you chose not to go on to college, is there hope of following your core passions? Of course, you can find a new group of people who are like the passionate you. How do I do that, you ask?

If you are one that loves to travel and would like to live in an entirely new place or experience an entire different environment  from where you grew up, go ahead; college will wait till you know what you want, finding new experiences and gaining new perspectives while seeking out new lifestyles and places that appeal to your inner spirit. Now that is real learning, the kind you will never have in a purely academic environment. In all of my travels around the world, it has given me a thousand times more desire for history, geology, and other people's culture. What can you learn in college sitting at a table in the library, going to parties, and listening to those who teach what they have never experienced? Volunteer somewhere until you become a

Les designing Urban City Planning for the Upper Nile State, in Malakal, South Sudan with Nigerian UN Representative September 2010 & September 2011. Nile Palace Hotel on the Nile River.

*"What a great person Les is. He is thoughtful and a great friend. He is enthusiastic with projects and assists those who are in need. I'd work with Les anytime."*

**– Anna Easteden**,
Nominated Actress,
Fashion Model,
Spokes Person,
Hollywood, CA
From Finland.

Anna was my guest at my nomination to the 2008 Hollywood Music Awards. Shown here modeling in front of my Xtra Lite Display Red Carpet display at the Adobe Theatre complex.

necessity and they hire you. You will find that what you are drawn to do even without the incentive of a big paycheck may be exactly what you really want to do, what pulls you and makes your heart realize a fresh breath coming from one of your core passions. You just don't know how to go about getting there so you can earn the necessary monetary rewards. Possibly after your travel experiences, you will find that what you really like requires some specific training or a rare degree you never thought of before. Isn't it remarkable that you now have the right perspective to go to school to get the training for something you really love to do and want to achieve that compensates you with more than money and satisfies your inner desire for life and fulfills your core passion.

Now, you can attend a specific school or go to a college with a real zeal and passion to achieve what your heart and soul has already experienced and what you now know really pleases you deep inside. If you can come to this kind of conclusion, you will work at something the rest of your life, and you will *Never* really need self-motivation or believe that you should be paid or something that you derive so much joy and fulfillment from.

It's simply your choice who you choose to befriend, but if you make friends where you love the work or are working with those who want to achieve the same goals, then you will find that their steel with sharpen your steel and together you will both be better off. This person you will always wish to allow them to teach you and their influence will be out of trust and admiration and thanksgiving for their lives. On the other hand, if you choose to hang around with people who maintain lifestyles you are not comfortable with, then they will be influencing you to destroy your moral fabric, bringing you down. If you remain silent and are afraid to stand up to them with your true beliefs, you run the risk of being shunned from the group. If you maintain these less-than-honest friendships, it just becomes much harder to break it off at a point in time when you finally come to your senses, and there are greater entanglements involved it is a guarantee that someone will always get hurt in these kind of relationships. There is no easy way out.

***Rule of thumb for you:*** if every step closer to their lifestyle just stretches you and you are learning to go forward one more step closer to your desired goal you have set for yourself, then good; you are moving into a relationship that will be beneficial to you. If you find that you just keep sliding down the salmon ladder of life and your goals are not being obtained, then **STOP** and make decisions for yourself. You are human, and humans will make occasional mistakes in their choices in life. Yes, you may fail, but you need to get up as in the case of the Ninja Warriors, who with a smile dry themselves off after they hit the water and adjust their strategy and their clothing and breathe a breath of fresh air, and give it one more go to win this time!

When you do make it to this different or higher level, however, you are now among a different and more inspiring group of people who are winners. Not those who want to see you succeed rather than fall into an easy, sloppy lifestyle of possibly drugs, sex, and alcohol, which will only bring you to a life of ruin and total defeat, misguidance, and unfortunately, extreme unhappiness or set you back or possibly lose your life or limit your life through an unforeseen tragedy.

Most people who are or on their way or even have become successful don't live their lives like everyone else, do they? Try the superrich, for instance; they certainly don't want to do anything to return to where they may have originated from. Perhaps their motivation was a life of poverty or servitude to rich parents who treated them like they owned them and set their course for them without any choices or decision on their part. These types of individuals end up either *"tubing out"* or getting hooked on drugs or like some daughters or sons of the well-known, who turn a blind eye on their parents' legacy and choose to be seen acting out as loose sex objects on YouTube and lower themselves publicly to demean or destroy their inheritance or spite its grip on them. Most, I suppose, are just bored with life because they can afford to do just about anything. The very idea of having gobs of money without regard to how hard it took or what their parents did to make it is a major tragedy. Not just for their parents, but for them also, being unable to make solid plans for their own futures before they spin out of control in destructive lifestyles.

The superrich hope to never return to poverty, a normal middle-class life, and in the end, they become what they desire not to be —a total failure and possibly lose all they once had or would inherit in the process in very self-destructive lifestyles.
I have witnessed too many cases on news reports or in Hollywood, New York City, or Washington DC in extreme cities across our country and around the world.
The other side of the pendulum are the ones that have found who they are and find their motivation and passion in life and leave their strong family attachments and desires and strike out on their own, leaving behind the arrogance, chains, and abuse of their parents or families. They no longer have to live in the shadow of their well-known or superrich parents or siblings. I am not saying that either of these scenarios leads to any form of happiness and fulfillment here, just that these scenarios certainly exist today in more abundance in our society. Super frustrated that they are rarely treated with a dose of reality and live daily in pain, not being able to do anything significant or genuine for themselves.
They are trapped in their own world they have created for themselves; and self-abuse, they believe, is there way out. Not at all; it is only a pain filled self-deception that leads to there destruction.

Les painting a portrait of his friend and pastor, Gil Maple and had the chance to give it to him six months before he passed away.

Most of them that obtain quick wealth also find they achieve the other side of true happiness, which may lead to a quick and early death due to the abuse and pressure from having sold their souls to those who control them. It's sad, but also extremely common among the superrich, talented musicians, artists, and those who wish to spend their lives in pursuit of being rich and well-known. What if you were raised in a home and found out at a young age that your parents were no longer going to live together? You may feel that the legs of your life have been kicked out from under you. How do you continue? It is the same; you must choose. After all, it is your life and not the mess your parents or siblings left you with. You have the ability to move on by getting to know what your real strengths are, find your own self-image, and obtain the inner strength you will need to rise above the situation you were presented with rather than live it out in regret and self-destruction. Getting to know who you are and finding your core passions are that which will bring you to your personal joy and satisfaction in your life.

## Where Do Your Passions Come From?

I'll bet you have never asked yourself why you are here, or maybe you did, so what's your answer? Did you know that everyone has a very specific calling in their life? Could you stand up right now and tell a group of ten, one hundred, or one thousand people what that one thing is for you? If you can't, then it is time to *STOP*, sit down, take that smartphone out of your ear and face, and put it down. Now, actually take even a few moments and try to focus on that lost person you have never met—it's *YOU!*

Even if you have no active faith, relationship, or acknowledge God in your life, you must admit that someone or something other than your mom and dad had something to do with designing and equipping your life.

The Bible clearly states that God has formed you in your mother's womb and knows and counts all the hairs on your head; he probably is one that knows you extremely well, surprisingly possibly even more intimately than your birth mother and father.



*"Before I formed you in the womb I knew you, before you were born I set you apart; I appointed you as a prophet to the nations."*

*(Jeremiah 1:5, New International Version (NIV))*

Have you ever thought of asking him? Yes, that three-ton gorilla in the room; you know very well who I am referring to—God. Do you think for a moment that the answers are found for your questions at some other planet? Another religion? A new form of yoga? The greatest new app? No, my friend, let me save you years of going the wrong direction in search of things that will NOT satisfy you ever!

The real answers to your life's questions are found in confronting your Maker and Creator God and Father who loves you. Wouldn't it be extremely clarifying and potentially empowering for you to experience the fullness of your purpose and life? Maybe even the kind of equipment, abilities that you already possess built in you? Even more the exact purpose for which you were designed and were brought to this earth and the exact mission your Creator God has for you? If you sincerely wish to find out He is not far away, He is always just one prayer away.

> ### *"Here I am! I stand at the door and knock. If anyone hears my voice and opens the door, I will come in and eat with that person, and they with me."*
>
> *(–Rev. 3:20, New International Version (NIV))*

Are you ready to spend some time with Jesus in your prayer closet or a quiet place in your mind that you can access at any time and come face-to-face, seeing yourself inviting Jesus Christ to come and speak with you? Who better to ask than the Creator God of the universe as to what exactly His divine purpose and calling is for your life and career. Continue with an attitude of becoming the clay that you are made of— sifted, patted down and firm, and waiting for the touch of the master Imagineer's hand. As the master creator of the universe allow His hands to reach in and touch you deeply molding you in to his marvelous creative work of art. Exquisitely empowering and imparting His divine vision enlightening and encouraging your future with hope.

Les LaMotte's Painting of Jesus part of a larger 4'x8' canvas for CrossPoint Evangelical Free Church, Bloomington, Minnesota.

## Discovering Your Core Passions

### Your Core Skills, Passions, and Role

The following exercise will take you through a series of simple questions about yourself; see if when you answer them, it helps you realize just an example of what taking the core passions assessment is all about—and it is not based on your friend, your parents, future employers, your special person but on your giving yourself honest answers. There are NO wrong answers, only ones that reveal your inner motivations and resources you never knew how to mine before.
What are the words or things people always tell you are good at or that they like about you?

*Some Examples:*
• You're good at organization.
• You're a leader, when no one else shows up to lead.
• You're detailed, and you can fight through any project before you generally with complete success well above everyone else.
• You interact and socialize well.
•  You're exciting to be around.
•  You communicate through your heart, your mind, and your soul.
• You love to have fun and play jokes on others.
•  Life is too serious, and you are here to make much more fun.
•  What are the things you have experienced in life so far that have been extremely fun and exciting?
• Focus on these, and you will never work the rest of your life!

### *(Bob Buford addresses the issue of purpose in his book, Halftime)*

Psalm 139 teaches us that we are fearfully and wonderfully made by the hands of a loving Creator. That creative process did not stop at childbirth. God has been molding and shaping you over the years with a care that exceeds that of the most meticulous craftsman. He put you in a unique family, He gave

4

you a unique personality, He has given you unique abilities, and He has woven a unique assortment of motivators into the very fabric of your life. God made you absolutely unique for a purpose.

> *"Most of us spend the first half of our lives becoming adults, getting an education and seeking our own version of 'success.' He then provides a clarion call to pursue lives of significance—of higher purpose. His message has resonated with many of us because we inherently recognize that true meaning is found somewhere, "beyond the pursuit of success."*

The fundamental principle that all believers share in any discussion of meaning and significance is the call to love and serve Christ by loving and serving others. However, a deeper sense of significance may be eluding you because you have not had the opportunity to focus your life work around a clear understanding of your God-ordained distinctive contribution.

## Focus on Your Life's Passion in the World!

In the earlier exercise, you will notice that I never said to ask your boss or anyone or coworker in your company—because **THEY DON'T** matter to you. Knowing and learning your core passions only matters to you. So this is the key to all success in life—make sure you are in charge, helping and guiding yourself through all the changes and demands put upon you by others or your family, using your passions as self-reinforcement to stay on track so that ultimately, you and God are satisfied with the results of your life.

Live with the full consciousness that anything can happen with no fear because God, your Heavenly Father, has designed you, and knows exactly all of your needs and how to deal with your desires because he cares for you. There are no guarantees, and you remain subject to all the possible earthly calamities, but the fire that you go through reassures you that they are there only to refine you so that you become your best you.

So it is here that your positive and helpful response to anything he puts in your pathway; as they say, what doesn't kill you makes you stronger, but hopefully not just *"harder."*

Remember to offer all of your plans to God and be ready for him to validate your decisions along the way. In my life, I practice the presence of Jesus in my life so your need for constant validation does not have to be interrupted with the stereotypes of getting alone, grabbing your Bible, and going into your prayer closet somewhere. As we are more mobile today, like you, I may find it best to take my "prayer closet" with me. Simply, stop, take a moment, slip into that quiet zone that is comfortable for you in your full presence of mind and heart to appreciate God's living presence

right there with you instead of struggling through every storm or bump in the road on your own. God never intended it for you to live your life in a vacuum without him; after all, He created you. If you take the time to present your whole plan to him and ask for his input on it, you allow Him to shed his almighty prospective and design. By simply listening and agreeing together will set it into motion. I speak from experience that every

Xtra Lite Display's Gift of a Heart Shaped Exhibit for the Children's Heart Link – at the Mall of America, Bloomington Minnesota.

4

plan that God reveals to you is always the winning one for you. Plans are just that, plans, and like laws, they are made to challenge and in some cases are broken in order to fulfill your ultimate required success. Don't let others tell you how to live or how to plan your life—simply seek God's wisdom, and He will be your personal and strong partner. However, be certain you stay close, daily walking with him on the path that He has chosen and placed you on.

My friend, that means that you and you alone can determine if you are a success no matter how many pokes and jabs you take from others. You are the master of your own destiny; don't make the mistake of being a *"people pleaser"* and a *"selfless loser."* This will destroy your own self-image and may take a great deal of time to reconnect or reorient your thinking, lessening your passion and purpose for being here. Strengthen your self-image and maintain your self-respect by staying on your course, holding your head high when things fall around you. Not because you are some sort of superstar, but because you have your silent partner. Guard your decisions for living and feeling love, peace, patience, kindness, self-control for these are the fruit of the Spirit and have no laws written against them. If you operate in them, granting full respect to your neighbor, you will be seen as a wonderful leader of men and women. Staying the course of your life, self-discovery, and planning for your future will drive you deeper to a path of self-freedom, honesty, and transparency to those

Full Back-wall Display for John Glenn's Speech at the Astronaut Candidate Press Conference Nation Space Agency of Japan Tokyo, Japan

around you and to God. You will literally excel in everything you do, desire, and work toward. In the end, you will have your personal joy and peace, and as love abounds from within you, there is no stopping the Glow and the Glory of God to shine brightly on your face. This is what people will see and respond to positively and with the grace He will grant you to succeed.

*"A few years back when I suddenly found myself separated from my job . . . you offered me a position at Xtra Lite Displays® in its early growth years. Having been roommates in college and both Eagle Scouts, and your best man, this was our chance to support each other and further our fellowship and common faith in Christ. I loved coming in each day always working on solutions to challenges we faced together in developing the business. Thank you, for inviting me to be part of Xtra Lite Displays®, it will remain a high lite of my life."*

George French,
roommate / confidant
at
Moorhead State University,
1970–1973

Moorhead University Entrance in Moorhead Minnesota / Fargo North Dakota

## Discovering the Lost Art of Self-Evaluation

### Honest Assessment

Without an honest assessment of who you really are and the motivations that direct you we tend to head off in some crazy self seeking journey until we finally can't handle our job, our station in life, and our house full of children and yet we are still searching for passion and purpose. Eventually you begin searching to find that special person or guru who you think will speak into your heart while what they really want is the keys to your wallet. They try to convince in the same manner as those frustrating long online video's trying to sell you something and they never seem to come to any conclusion at the end. You look under every rock only to find another home grown philosophy to *"find yourself."* However, you find out much later that they are just another new version of a *"snake oil salesperson."* All they want is to fix some cracks and patch up our lives and add another coat of paint while turning off our inner voice and the flame to God begins to die. The distractors increase their vibe that keeps us listening to their helter-skelter worldly ramblings until we need to get that wild new hairdo, a new set of pure linen cloths, and become a vegan while learning a new *"Far Eastern"* philosophy. We as Americans tend to be easy prey and buy into all of that mystical thinking and jump in hook, line, and sinker and they have us. After a long exhaustive search and not having found any real truth in too long, we just head off to our next adventure, still not knowing who we are or the core passions that motivate us. If we just took a minute sat down and openly consulted with God for a few minutes a day we would find out who we really are and why He created us in the first place. Our true identity and core passions could have been revealed to us and resolved dozens of years sooner and for a lot less waste of time and money. The simple truth is that our heavenly Father God wants to give us Himself and set us free through an honest relationship with His son Jesus Christ, who paid the price for our sins and wants to communicate His value and passions He has already given us. But, we resist and trip over the word sin; it seems the world and ourselves have thrown that reality out years ago. We excuse it based on a half heartily trying and without complete success we just tossed the concept out. We tell ourselves we tried before and it just didn't work. We tried it on our own and no longer see it as a solution so we continue to believe the lie from the pit of hell. This is where the lie that we keep holding onto comes from. The truth is that we are sinful and powerless in ourselves to clean ourselves up to stand before a Holy God. God doesn't want us to become sinless; he wants to provide us the gift of Jesus Christ to eliminate our sin condition eternally with his divine power and authority and shower us with the love and righteous of Jesus Christ. Have you asked yourself who have I waited so long to answer that knock at my hearts door from Jesus?

## Finding Your Core Passions

If you don't look, you don't find—it is that simple. Most people just don't have the time of day, or they use that as an excuse to not take the time because of the immediate demands and pressures of the world around them. They have allowed others or themselves to become too busy running off to make more money, go to their cabins, take care of their children, fish, or just drink their lives away and spend their hard-earned money in casinos, bars, or clubs or at home at excessive entertainment computer games. Now, I didn't say you have to take a vow of poverty or celibacy. Learning what it means to have and grow daily a genuine righteous life in Jesus. To enjoy the fruit of His attitude toward others, it is a constant battle of keeping Him on the throne of your lives. His winning ways and attitude of love is completely evident throughout his recorded life in the New Testament Gospels, *"Good News"* of the Bible.

Jesus doesn't ask you to forget about your dreams and desires; on the contrary, it is through your devotion to Him that you will gain the power to help others and be obedient to His calling. He grants you rewards of further gifting and the power to be an overcomer here so that you can continue to serve Him with more impact to an even a broader audience and influence of people. The result for me with our *"Men with a Mission"* was Sonrise a New Tomorrow, an album of my nine original songs I shared in prison ministry. God's blessing with my music has just broadened and continues ministering to a whole new group of youth. As of last month, I have won eight major music awards for my album, individual specific songs, and collaborative works, including two international awards. My music is available on all distribution sites worldwide or LesLaMotte.com which contains bio's, stories, blog, and other sheet music and books about writing and writing music.

**The Great Physician**
Best Christian Gospel
Song • May 2017

**Sonrise A New Tomorrow**
Best Christian Gospel
Album • June 2018

**Sonrise A New Tomorrow**
© 1993 First Released
**Sonrise**
© 2019 Release
Nine Original Songs by
**Les LaMotte, Lyrics by
Les LaMotte, Vicky LaMotte,
and Peter Reese.**
Produced by the late
Lonnie Knight
Mosquito Shoals Recording
Studio, Minneapolis.

**Sonrise A New Tomorrow**
Worship Artist of the Year • June 2007

It is absolutely amazing what God will do when your heart is attuned to His heart and plan for your life. If we think we have it all together and do it our own way, it will all turn to ashes and dust as the scripture says, and it does, believe me. To walk the road of Jesus, you have to see everyone around you as having individual worth, equal creatures of God's design and love. Jesus didn't heal a crowd; no, he dealt with individuals. They simply brought their wounds and wounded that needed healing, their minds of insanity, and their bodies and minds filled with lust and sin, and even demons. Jesus never turned away from anyone and always spoke to them with grace and peace and accepted their place in life without disgracing them, but rather by asking them to simply follow Him.

*"So what is the true essence of passion? To me, it is having that deep yearning inside of you that will do anything to be expressed. It's a key that will lead you to your purpose and a life of fulfillment."*

## *"You know passion when you see it."*

*It's the athlete who is up at five every morning working out to hone their muscle memory. It's the artist who enters a flow-like state, cutting themselves off from this reality to create in another. It's the CEO or entrepreneur who day after day consistently does whatever it takes to bring their A-game no matter how many times they get knocked down. It's the ballet dancer, musician, and actor who study from the best, are told no again and again as they work to better themselves to compete in a world that is full of people with gifts. Passion. It's the fuel that gives a seemingly normal person superpowers. Passion is what gets them up every morning. Passion is what fuels their mind, body, and spirit when the people around them are taking the path of least resistance or doing what everyone else does. Passion is what sparks their creative genius to live in a world of possibility. Passion is what carries them over the threshold of mediocrity when they show up."*

*(–Rebecca Kirson, author / life coach, YourSacredTruth.com) used by permission.*

Many people and churches try to gum up the Gospel and think that you must add tons of stuff to it to make it legitimate or relevant to today's lifestyles. This is a fallacy on their part; the Gospel of Jesus Christ is easy, simple, and it has not changed in over two thousand years. You don't have to be a seminary-trained preacher or theologian with eight years of schooling and a master of divinity degree to share Christ's purpose and truth with others. No, it was meant for every believer to deliver in the words of their own testimony—their own view of the car accident of life, from their perspective, and this cannot be taken away from them or supposed by others to be incorrect. It is their personal touch point or fingerprint of the Savior in their life, and no one else has it, knows the details of it, nor can use it against them or deny that it took place. In fact, if not told by them to others, it will never be revealed and therefore be rendered inactive and of no earthly or heavenly good, and it will simply go to the grave with them instead of reaching others who could discover and fully connect to Jesus Christ as their Savior and Lord.

However, for those who were trying to sell and trade money for their own wealth in His Father's house or the people's place of worship of God, he did not give the same grace and peace but rather turned over the tables and scattered the unclean money and idols in total disgust and agony for the abuse and shaming they had made His Father's house of prayer.

Adam and Eve's offense against God in the Garden of Eden put us all in jeopardy and made us unacceptable to a righteous and Holy and Righteous God. Since God is righteous and He is without sin, and though He created us, He can't accept us because we are tainted with the sin of Adam being born of the flesh. In God's great wisdom, He knew we would sin and fall away from him because it was the only way to prove to us that we had the free will to choose. He knew we are weak in our sin, and He already planned from the beginning of the universe for our redemption in his only son Jesus. Jesus isn't a fictionalized character, a goody-two shoes, a religious leader, pastor, religious freak, tax collector, or a well-meaning business person; yet He hung around with all of them.

Why, because He wanted to share with them the way to their full redemption through accepting His free gift of salvation in Him.

*"He still stands and knocks at the door of our hearts to receive Him today so we can accept him as our Lord and Savior. With the sealing of His Holy Spirit in us, He guides us to become fully righteous in God's sight. Not because of our goodness, but because of God's son Jesus as the righteous perfect lamb that was sacrificed as the payment for all who believe in Him. He paid in full the penalty for our sin nature, setting us free to serve our Father God."*

(*– Les LaMotte • Imagineer*)

This is what I mean when I say that I took the road less traveled by, as the road that Jesus has asked us to walk today seems so offensive to people in general around the globe. Why so offensive? Because they would rather believe that following after Him is simply a story, that only mad men and women listen to His foolishness, a waste of time, or perhaps there is another way, person, ideology with more options of those who have tried to make themselves out to be super religious by their godless self-destructive acts and traditions of self-mutilation and strict law keeping. However, they are all without the proof of the full payment of Jesus

Les and Stephen's First project for the people of South Sudan under Sudan Hope organization. *"The Boat of Hope"* which begin in 2001 and launched in Gambella Ethiopia on July 17, 2003. Here it is sitting in dry dock in Matar Ethiopia where I took this picture on my way to Stephen's village of Maker by boat. It literally saved over 250,000 lives during the original conflict in South Sudan.

demonstrated in history by His gruesome and horrible death and resurrection from the dead. Jesus, despite what people say today, is still alive with God at his right hand in heaven. How do we know this to be true? Because He has given His Holy Spirit to each true believer that embodies Jesus and the love that He and only He alone has ever demonstrated in this world. Why serve a dead man or idol of silver or gold? We serve a living God who cares for us, wants us to have a personal and vital relationship with Him on a daily basis, and has provided for us with a future and a hope.

> ***"For I know the plans I have for you,"
> declares the Lord, "plans to prosper you
> and not to harm you, plans to give you
> hope and a future ."***
>
> *(–Jeremiah 29:11 New International Version (NIV))*

> ***"It is said that we can live about 40 days
> without food, about three days without
> water, about eight minutes without air, but
> only for one-second without hope ."***
>
> *(Unknown)*

### *What the world needs now is love sweet love.*

The extremely talented, prolific, and versatile Jackie DeShannon was one of the first successful *American* female singer/songwriters to hit the rock and pop music scene back in the '60s.

I say right on, Jackie; they need love sweet love, however they are looking for it in all the wrong places.

## *All You Need is Love*

*(–The Beatles, one of the most listened-to and purchased songs.)*

Even the Beatles knew that all we need is love, and yes, it is all we need—however, not the sexual or erotic love they speak of here, but the love of Jesus who died on our behalf so that we might be made acceptable to God so we can experience His full love that once one drinks of it, he will never thirst again.

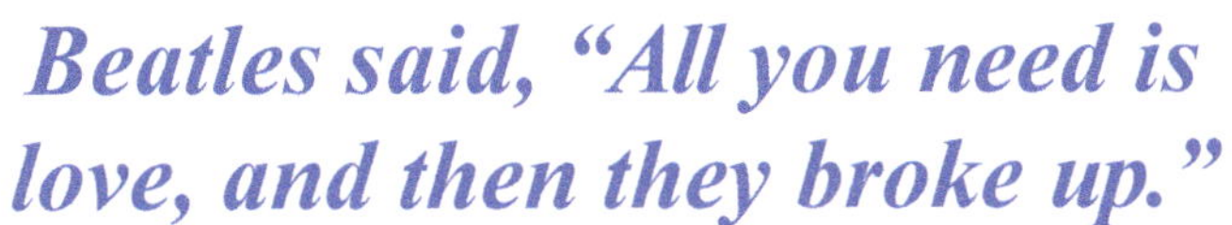


## *Beatles said, "All you need is love, and then they broke up."*

*(–Larry Norman, singer/songwriter, pioneer of Christian rock'n roll)*

Yes, Larry, you are so right here; the world just goes around proclaiming that we need love, but it has no real knowledge of the source of where it comes from or who is the author of the love we seek. Not the love we try to create in ourselves, which just ends in total failure, because it is not based on anything real and therefore lacks the power and authority to bind us together like glue rather than cause trouble and defy and deny God's power to produce His love in us.

## *My command is this: "Love each other as I have loved you. Greater love has no one than this: to lay down one's life for one's friends."*

*(–John 15:12–13, New International Version (NIV))*

***All You Need Is Love*** one of the Beatles' best-known and loved songs in recent history with its full production HD sound. Every day, we hear bands and dancers troops shouting out the answer on the radio, our smartphones and in stadiums and malls asking the question with no answers—and we fall completely into their hands while we love, appreciate, and perhaps mindlessly worship the songs and the songsters and their extremely empty songs. Today's songs have almost no words, or too much foul cuss words that distinguish and dumb you down. Modern music is more like a wall of sound with a beat with two notes that is definitely not in praise and worship of our righteous God, but of self-made gods with evil designs entirely opposite of the one true God of heaven. He has demonstrated His sacrificial death of His Son Jesus on behalf of every man and all we are required to do is receive Jesus and acknowledge His gift to us and in return for our obedience He promises us eternal life.

It's as if the entire planet has been set adrift. The masses are now under a spell of evil and thoughtlessness; they are just plain ignorant of the true love that Jesus has died to obtain for them. They can only see Him as a myth, a mad man's dream, and totally fail to recognize Jesus as the author of truth, perfecter of love, and the one that holds everything even the atoms of the universe together with his own hands. Our only requirement is to recognize Jesus for whom He is, Savior and Lord of our lives. We need to make that decision of faith now to change our own will or we can wait as the Bible says until all men will have to bow their knee to Him and receive their judgment by Him. However, Christ's salvation will no longer be offered to you then, and His free gift of love will no longer be able to recycle your corrupt sin filled heart and set you free. Today is the day of salvation… open your hearts door and invite Him in while there is still time for you to receive His everlasting love!

> ***"Therefore, since we have been justified through faith, we have peace with God through our Lord Jesus Christ."***
>
> *(–Romans 5:1, New International Version (NIV))*

## My South Sudan Connection

### Giving Back

Just before 9/11, I was ministering in music at an International Church in North Minneapolis. When I finished, this tall black man from the back row simply walked up to me and said, *"My people need you."* After that, Stephen Khor Chambang and I became instant friends, and we began to see how I could use my insight, influence, and resources of my person and company to help these war-torn people of South Sudan.

We proceeded by counseling groups of Nuer refugee former soldiers—now the seed of developing political leaders of South Sudan including the Vice President, Dr. Riek Machar, hosting meetings in our business offices and traveling to Ames, Iowa, and Omaha, Nebraska, in their initial years of coming to the United States. I hired and taught Stephen how to solder and build our custom lighting at Xtra Lite Displays. He brought our Xtra Lite Display back to his home of Maker, in South Sudan, for a regional rally during the ongoing war there. Together, Stephen and I have planned and met in his home village in 2009. In 2010, I was invited to work in Malakal, the capital city of the Upper Nile State of South Sudan for several months as an Urban Planner. In Matar, Ethiopia, his mother Elizabeth and her three daughters have taken on eighty-nine children that they rescued from the last uprising in South Sudan on December 15, 2013, when twenty thousand Nuer South Sudanese were killed in the streets of their capital city of Juba by their own government. Months following

Stephen Khor Chambang, South Sudanese/American and Les LaMotte President / CEO of Xtra Lite Displays, Burnsville Minnesota in Les's corporate office after we met July 4, 2001.

that, they attacked and killed five hundred thousand in a northern village near the oil wells and caused approximately four-thousand refugee children to pour through the small village of Matar Ethiopia. We have struggled to try to send a few dollars each month to keep them all alive. They are constantly in need of seed, medical supplies, and other living expenses. These children have not had a roof over their head for about five years as the house that Stephen built for his family, one of the best in the village at the time, simply fell apart as most stick houses do and must be rebuilt. However, we have not been able to raise the funds to build these refugee children a house.

Les LaMotte and Stephen Khor Chambang, Co-Founders of Sudan Hope at Minnesota Senator Coleman's Office in Washington DC July 24, 2003

The result is many coming down sick with malaria because they don't have any protection from the mosquitos in the summer wet season. We have a huge farmland of over 250 acres of tillable land by the river, but we need to buy seed, which must be planted by hand by his family with very few crude tools. We have twenty-five head of cattle, but they are not enough to provide the amount of milk needed for the children. Would you please consider providing these eighty-nine children a *hope for a future?* Please support our work in Matar and Gambela, Ethiopia, where there are about 750,000 South Sudanese

Xtra Lite Displays in Stephen's home village of Maker in South Sudan for a community celebration.

that have come as refugees for over twenty-five years. Give us the ability to go and bring structure, leadership, and incubate many new business opportunities to help them become the best that they can be. (EastAfricaComDev.org).

*"I met Les LaMotte in Upper Nile, South Sudan in 2010 when he was working on Urban Planning for the city of Malakal. As Director for the Administration in the Ministry of Infrastructure and Rural Development. I worked closely with him on his Urban planning project. Les is a down to earth trustworthy fellow who has a great sense of humor. He is smart, a team player, and above all has proven to be a good friend and support to the people of South Sudan for the last two decades."*

*(–Reat Nhial Tuany, South Sudanese / American, Rochester, New York)*

*My South Sudan Connection*

6

Les consulting with the US National Nuer Community Development Services, *NCDS.org* in Jackson, Minnesota USA – January 12, 2019.

Les and Stephen have developed a new organization East African Community Development with a plan to teach the making of solar and solar chargers for the people of South Sudan now refugees in Gambella, Ethiopia.

# Yearly Evaluation to Move Forward With Your Dream!

## The Results of Not Understanding Who You Are…

From my personal professional experience, I spent about five to six years working inside other companies. That leaves almost forty years I worked for myself doing what I loved. Fulfilling my passion for art, design, and even music. In conversations with many of my peers, I ask them what discipline they graduated from college in. They all end up telling me a long sad story of how they never went into their discipline they studied for. I believe from my experience that it was almost 80 percent of them revealed to me that they had to discover their passion and retool for what they now realize what true passion is, like instead of psychology, they moved on to photography or something wildly different from the degree they received.

## Breakout of the Frozen Chosen

The late pastor and worldwide motivational speaker and author Myles Munroe whom I met at a conference in the Bahamas and I became a quick fan stated that *"Chinese never enter a town and ask where can I get a job. They ask where can I make a difference and set out to build a company or service that specifically meets the needs in that community. Have you ever seen them fail? They never open a business alone; they go to their guanxi group and collect the money they need to buy everything in cash so there is no interest in their overhead but to repay their guanxi group."*

*See, I have refined you, though not as silver; I have tested you in the furnace of affliction. For My own sake, I do this. How can I let Myself be defamed? I will not yield My glory to another".*

(–Isaiah 48:1-11, New International Version (NIV))

## How do you wish to spend your life currency?

Live like you are planning what they will say about you.
- What is it that I want others to absolutely know about me when I am gone?
- What do I want to leave as my legacy after I'm not here?
- Write the words on your epitaph or your tombstone you want everyone to know about you.

## Setting Your Personal Goals

After you consider your yearly personal goals, identify what in each of the five passions you are going to work on and where you want to be with them in one year. Write your answers to them down and seal it in an envelope marked *"Open One Year from this Day."* Include the date.

In one year, open it up and then sit down with a close friend and read it together to see how well you have done. Your friend or coworker can possibly give you some prospective on how you have done. Repeat this process every year for the rest of your career. This will remind yourself that you are first working for changing your habits, tendencies, and your destiny.

It will help you to include and consider your core passion in every decision you make and how you spend your life. This small exercise will ultimately affect your outcome for years to come. Observe and write down your thoughts and seal it up for another year with additional things you wish to further improve on. You will eventually see your family and those who love and care about you begin to acknowledge the changes that you are working on. Continue to be the clay in the potter's hands and allow God to mold you into what he has created you to be completely. Your life will be a testimony to everyone you meet that you are who you exactly are meant to be. You!

*"Make it they will come. Whoop it up!*
*Shout about it, tell everyone! Give back.*
*Leverage your cash and spend it wisely.*
*Make your money work hard for you.*
*Make decisions with your spouse or special*
*friend's wise counsel with a fresh perspective."*

(– *Les LaMotte • Imagineer, 2018*)

## Use Your Audience Lifeline

Listen to many wise counselors and then make your decision. Never make a decision or spend a huge amount of money





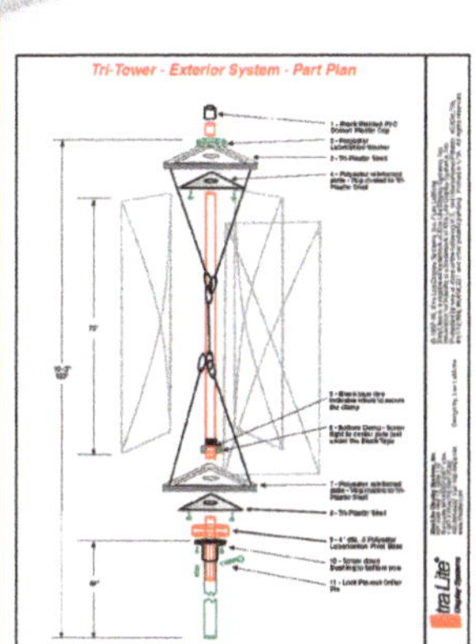


Outdoor Graphical
Turning Towers
Daytona 500 for
Mobil 1 Racing Team
Mechanical and
Structural Design
by Les LaMotte.

without sleeping on it first. Take the time to think it through. Take the time to make important decisions. Inform others who you respect well before you pull the trigger.

## I Took the Road Less Traveled By . . .

*"I took the road less traveled by,"* to quote Robert Frost, who is one of the most-famous and best-read poet, well-known at least in my boomer gen. However, I am not sure that it's even read today in classrooms or for the last twenty years as it doesn't fit the present-day narrative. It asks us to decide where are you going. This kind of personal retrospect is not necessarily what is on top of people's minds today. The modern mind finds self-reflection and awakening to their core passions being tied to God's equipping and personal mission for each person as hard to comprehend.

I know my children were all taught in grade school through high school that they had to work in groups or teams. Although it is true in life, it is just slightly twisted by disconnecting our children's interest in entrepreneurial pursuits of the American Dream. Rather what is expected today regardless of their intellectual ascension or IQ number are individuals using their God-given talents to forge their own way despite all the others around them to rise to the highest level that is possible for them. I fought very hard to help my children see and experience it in action. I worked in my home design studio as a freelance graphic designer for most of my career. My children observe for themselves the advantages as a countermeasure to these groupthink concepts taught in school. I know that my children have caught these ideas and principles functioning as much happier, healthier, and more productive young men and women, now valuable adults because of both I and my wife's examples. Standing out from the crowd is literally frowned on today. The masses no longer value the contribution of the individual who work with their hands and minds to produce the next breakthrough product or service. We are made to believe that only the corporate or government world can achieve anything of great importance today or for coming generations. This kind

Pencil Drawing by Les LaMotte at the Park in Burnsville Minnesota

of absurd thinking is part of the programmed dumbing down of America so that we will accept much less of ourselves. This kind of programming destroys our self-esteem, making us more subservient to those in authority over us who wish to control us and cut us off from our true image and inheritance as people of the Creator God.

One of the biggest scams today is to emphasize having a college or university degree or MBA in order to enter into the business world. This educational concept is simply untrue, and it has never been a requirement unless you wake up and smell the roses and realize that what others are trying to paint as your future is only an image of their utopian ideology. This mind-set actually results in the opposite for students and keeps them financially trapped by reducing their career choices distorting their worldview after graduation.

No one in their right mind can see the dwindling of family building and becoming skilled workers of every kind as a good direction or sustainable for our country's economic health and stability. We simply don't need any more ideologists; we need more pragmatists that get down and get dirty to engage and grapple with our society to form and shape it with true American ideals. Upholding our freedom by our constitutional rights, not sitting back in our ivory towers and plotting how to change everything so it fits our ideal or the insane inhumane dystopias while they set themselves up as gods destroying all that we have been founded upon. Sound like a bad movie? All you have to do is just look at the content of the movies that are being producing of late. That is a big clue as to what they want us to believe is coming.

### Wake up, America;

we do not have to just swallow this stuff. We are free; don't allow others to steal that freedom away from you. I guess my recent award-winning song from my album Sonrise a New Tomorrow says it best; it speaks of this present state of mindlessness we are presently living in. It asks the listeners a personal question: What will your response be?



7

Les LaMotte,
Junior Art Director -
Russ Reid Advertising,
Pasadena, CA
Visited WorldVision to
review photographs to
design an idealized
starving Child Graphic
used on Nationwide
TV Special Promoting
World Vision 1976

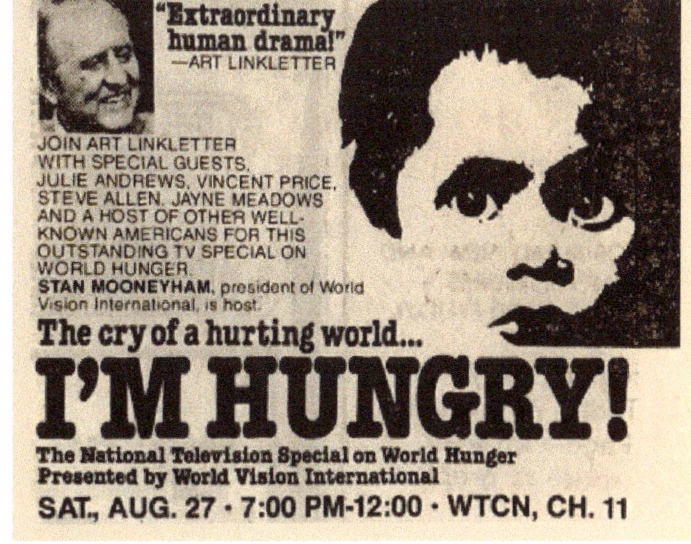

## Where Are You Goin'

*Music by Singer/Songwriter Les LaMotte*
*Lyrics by Les LaMotte & Peter Reese © 1993 ASCAP*

Where are you goin',
Is every direction the same?
Where are you goin',
Are you livin' in pain, are you livin' in pain?
Is there somebody who'll set you straight.
Gives you direction, and won't hesitate, who won't hesitate.
I've met somebody, who sees me goin' somewhere.
I trust somebody 'cause he really cares, yeah he really cares.
His name is Jesus, he's got a plan for your life.
He brings you direction, turns pain to delight,
He turns pain to delight.
Jesus is here now, we're ready to start, take the first step now.
Give him your heart, yeah, give Him your heart.
Come give him your heart, yeah,
Come give him your heart. Right now!

Awarded The Akademia's
Best Christian / Gospel
Album,  June 2018
*"Where Are You Goin'"*
was in heavy rotation on
30 online radio stations
around the world.

# Sonrise A New Tomorrow

## Spiritual Awakening

This road not taken, or should I say seldom taken, is definitely the road I have taken. First, I decided to follow the road to that of selflessness, just like the one Jesus demonstrated in his life of compassion, forgiveness, and grace to others.

How did I experience this in my life? After I went through some very upsetting times over the loss of my major position at Skyline Display due to false accusations. I was sitting in my design office in my basement, and I suddenly was struck by the piercing rays of the sun rising through the window. As this beam of sunlight shone brightly, I also heard a familiar voice on the radio station from KTIS, our local Christian radio. It was actually someone I knew personally, Dr. Chuck Swindoll, whom I had the pleasure of serving breakfast to at a retreat for men in Salem, Oregon, years before. He asked me to come and speak with him if I was ever in California.

What I didn't know at the time was that our former Bible study couple's wife from Madison, Wisconsin, had become his church secretary. She was showing us around and pointed out his office, and I caught his eye as he was leaving and he remembered our short discussion back in Oregon. He invited me to come into his office, and we had a few minutes of conversation. That particular day, Chuck's message over the radio hit me over the head, and I suddenly woke up and realized that God has provided the sun in the heavens as a sign of our need for recycling and renewing each day. In other words, every day we are on this planet, we may ask for Jesus to renew our body, mind, and soul. After hearing this as if for the first time, I was finally released from my doom and depression. I asked, *"Lord, what can I do to walk with you to bring this same enlightenment to others?"* I told my story of that special message I received that morning to a few of my church brothers. I asked them to pray with me so that God could give us his direction to move forward on his prompting to me personally, but also to all of us as brothers of our church. Someone suggested we form a band of brothers and go to



Dr. Billy Graham became the president of Northwestern Bible College in 1948. KTIS Radio became an immediate success and doubled the College's enrollment by the early 1950s.

prisons and proclaim the forgiveness and grace of Jesus. So we did just that, and we called ourselves the *"Men with a Mission"* and set out to lead in praise and worship music. Our mission included sharing the love of Christ to every prison inmate in Minnesota. We ministered together for about five years. After that, I did it mostly on my own for another five years, and not only in Minnesota, but also in 5 prisons in Tucson, Arizona and three south of Houston, Texas.

### *I Took the Road Less Traveled By*

*A poem by Les LaMotte*
*My apologies to Robert Frost.*

*It is said by men much wiser than I,*
*That they took the road less traveled by.*
*Well, it seems their road may have been different,*
*but lonely all the same.*
*Down my road was a lantern held high,*
*so each bump and hole in the road could be seen*
*and yet if it were not for the light there go I.*
*As I traveled I wandered from left then to right*
*and sometimes slipped ahead or behind of the light.*
*It was then that I questioned the path I was on*
*and wondered what fool I had followed and who's*
*path they were on.*
*The lantern it seemed undaunted by me*
*kept ever so steady in its mission to free all who*
*wavered like me.*
*As the path gave way to fields of wonder*
*other roads promised and yes, I did ponder.*
*I ran for the light the one I was under*
*and looking into its beacon of grace I grew and*
*I grew until I was stronger.*
*The lessons I've learned as I've traveled this trail*
*are many and rough and I've often failed,*
*but the lantern is still lit an old treasured friend.*
*So wiser I've become and wiser you'll be*
*if you take the road less traveled like me.*

How did giving to others in this way work out? When we first began our prison ministry, we were very idealistic and definitely naive, thinking that somehow we were going in to bring a great message and we were going to influence these poor men into trusting in Jesus Christ. What we discovered
was that the men in most prisons had already formed a sense of a local church group of believers and their stories of Christ changing them actually ministered to us even more. It certainly gave us a greater sense of strength after hearing many of their stories of how Christ had gotten their attention by being sentenced to prison. That gave them time to meet the person of Jesus Christ and how the Spirit of God released to them the resurrection power to enhance their experience while God worked in their hearts, transforming them into men of God so they could be released to a new life. We, on the other hand, realized that if not by the grace of God, we also could be in their position in prison. That is what they did or who they were; they were now sorry for what they had done and were hungry to learn what it means to serve Jesus Christ and live in his new way, first in prison and then when they are released.

Les's Painting
*"One Nation Indivisible?"*
Oil on Canvas
Winner of the 1973
"Best of Show"
Moorhead State
University

8

We spent many weekends in prisons with inmates reading and studying the Word of God together. The one time that stands out in my mind is when I was sitting at a table with five murders. One of the young men, only eighteen years old, seemed most disturbed.

I took him aside and asked him about his story, and then upon hearing it, I knew that his need for Christ was imminent and so I took my leather-bound Bible and gave it to him and told him it was now his.

That evening, he began to look into it and discovered a small booklet that was from Billy Graham's ministries. He read it and it asked him to hear the knocks of Jesus upon his heart and to respond by asking Jesus into his heart. Amazingly and thankfully, he did. The next day, he had a definite new sense of joy and had a smile on his face, and I barely could recognize it was the same young man. I asked him to share with our group what had taken place in his life to be able to allow us to see this kind of joy. He then told us the story of how he had found the booklet and he did what it instructed him to do. While his head was bowed in reverence to Christ and in an attitude of prayer, he simply thanked Jesus for dying on the cross for his sins and asked Jesus to come

Water Color by Les LaMotte, 1972
*"But even the archangel Michael, when he was disputing with the devil about the body of Moses, did not himself dare to condemn him for slander but said, "The Lord rebuke you!"*

*(– Jude 1:9 New International Version (NIV))*

8

into his heart and take up residency there. When he told the group of four other convicted murderers at the table, you could see that all of their eyes were welling up with tears for this young man, who finally felt at peace with God and ready to begin a new life in His grace and truth.

This rich experience that morning of seeing the peace that had come over this formerly troubled young man finally taught me the lesson of the power of Jesus to transform even the toughest and blackest of hearts and to begin walking with Jesus and serve others before themselves. Then I was asked to begin a new role of responsibility as a *"pen pal"* and mentor to a select number of individual inmates that were soon to be processed out of prison. I would visit them in prison on Saturdays and spend time talking, buy them a small refreshment, and reassure them of God's help through their upcoming release. Listen to their needs and pray with them over their concerns. Eventually, as they were placed in halfway houses, I was able to sign them out for a few hours and go and have some fun, enjoy a talking lunch discussing their future plans, and introduce them make a solid way back to their new life with Jesus outside the prison walls.

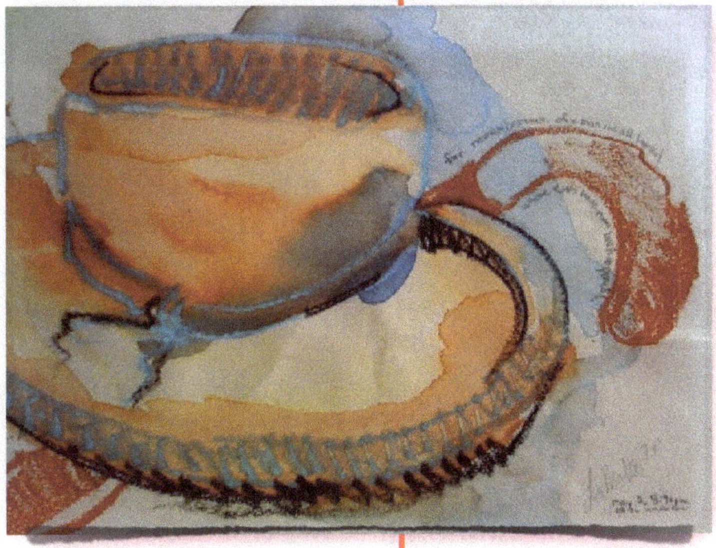

The stats at the time were for every inmate who professed a relationship with Jesus Christ and demonstrated it while serving their time, there was an 80 percent chance they would never return to prison. However, if they were released without a faith based relationship with Christ and weren't interested in this kind heart healing relationships, there was an 80 percent chance that they would reoffend and be back in prison. As Chuck Colson taught me, it actually makes real sense to expose incarcerated people to a loving Savior so that by making him Lord of their lives, there is actual real transformation.

Grandpa's Les's hat and cane painted for celebrating his passing.
*"For remembrance of a man we all loved whose eyes have now been opened!"*

Water Color, Oil Crayon, and Pastels by Les LaMotte, May 2,1970

## Passionate Imagineers

### Walt Disney, the Pioneer of Imagineering

Walt began at the turn of the century as a pioneer in the infancy of animation. He worked in several studios and showed great ambition and leadership even though through many turns of events and business bankruptcy. Did that somehow destroy his passion or his dream? Absolutely not! He just kept ongoing. One day, it suddenly dawned on him that it wasn't only about the cartoon characters and visuals on the screen at all but that there needed to be sounds, feelings, mystery, and people transported into a completely new place. Somewhere they had never

experienced before with tons of fantasy and fun—the concept for *Disneyland was born!* He probably hatched the idea as he personally went about building a backyard-sized scale-model railroad. I am sure he saw the smiles and fun on the faces of his neighbors and friends that he invited over as they experienced the wind on their face, sounds of the click and clack of the rails, and were stimulated by the pungent smell and smoke in their eyes of the locomotive. Yes, now this was the beginning of a total experience!

Upon conceiving the "*Vision of Disneyland*," he immediately went on the hunt for financial backing. Like all new ideas who are in search of a financial backer to exist, his timing couldn't have been better as it was only seven years since World War II ended and men and women returning from the war we're in search of anything new. There was a surge in the creation of jobs and businesses. Walt quickly realized that this was the right time, but where was he going to find the visionary backers to finance his dream and especially where would he find the creative group of engineers to design and build it?

Where would he get the vast amount of money to begin such a grandiose project? As with most outstanding artists with huge visions in history, he went to the only one he could convince that it would work and only one who *"saw the vision" and "knew the power of the visionary who had conceived of it,"* his brother Roy.

**On his death, journalism professor Ralph S. Izard commented that the values in Disney's films are those *"considered valuable in American Christian society,"* which include "individualism, decency, . . . love for our fellow man, fair play and toleration."**

After securing the financing to begin, the next question is where would he begin finding that talent pool of men and women who had the specific skills to begin to make his dream a reality? I'm sure he went out into the industrial marketplace and tried to find the companies who had a vast amount of technical skills to design and perform all these unusual techniques and work with exotic materials. They were just coming out of wartimes, and money was skinny. To have to invest their money, time, and personnel to do the R&D and tool up for his giant tasks, well, it was difficult for them to conceive. They simply could not put their companies in jeopardy of possible failure or loss of income just to make Walt's visions come into reality. He soon realized, like my experience with Skyline Displays® initial story, he had to grow a particular culture of highly technical, gifted, dedicated

Filming *"The Custom Alternative"* for Skyline Displays in 1988, for the release of the Formation® Display System at their Annual Meeting in Bloomington, MN. Les LaMotte, Design Director, Writer, and Executive Producer.

people who could work in tandem together and follow his very specific vision. They begin working together in a highly and creatively charged environment to achieve the fantasy and delight that was completely above everything ordinary they had ever seen or experienced.

Today, we can only observe the unbelievable result; he created not only a place but an entirely new culture of people, which became known as his *"Imagineers."* These hearty souls stepped off the train of normalcy and onto the train to *"Tomorrow Land"* with Walt! Eventually, this tight group of creative and engineering minds soon became known as the *"Walt Disney Imagineering Company."*

## Pursuing Your Childhood Dreams

I was just a youngster in the fifties, and Walt Disney had produced many new films and begun working on the Walt Disney theme park in Anaheim, California. I thought he walked on water, as I stared at the black-and-white TV soon to be in *"Living Color"* every Sunday night with the creative visuals and characters he created. He used the highest production values that were available at that time and some new ones he invented. As we all know Walt Disney's franchise exploded. His reputation in the minds of children everywhere saw him as their hero. I drank the Kool-Aid, and when I was in eighth grade, my family took a trip to Los Angeles to enjoy this world wonder and modern marvel known as the Walt Disney theme park. When you see something as amazing as

Custom Portable Display System and Graphic by Xtra Lite Displays launching the Disney Space Exhibit for the Epcot Center – 8' high by 18' long.

Disneyland the very first time you experience it makes a very huge impression on your life. So way back in my childlike mind, I felt a tug in my spirit, but at the time, I had no idea what it meant until almost fifty years later.

## Groupthink

I wonder how different our world would be if Steve Jobs, CEO and founder of Apple Inc., was told that individual thinking is wrong and that we must all believe in working together as one under the concept of *"groupthink."* Maybe there wouldn't be the explosion in the last ten years of Gen-Xers are not even aware of the brief history of their all-important "can't live without it technology", smartphones, pads, and light weight and portable laptops. Perhaps that they would never have been designed and made into an international base necessity and social culture opinion tools, if the Apple board of directors cut Steve's funding off for such projects and then released him from his own company. Where would Apple be today without an Imagineer like Steve Jobs? Where would the entire world be without this living miracle? Maybe there wouldn't be these absolute marvels of communications, computing, photography, and Facebook. How could all these radical ideas become a necessity of our youth and business who wouldn't have been able to invent and capture this huge market? Today, as I am writing this, Apple Inc. stock just hit one trillion, and that makes them the largest company ever on the NY stock exchange. They were bought by the Chinese; now there is another radical change of which Steven Jobs is responsible for even after his untimely death.

I am sure Steven Jobs read Robert Frost because he was also a product of the *"boomer gen"* like myself. One could say that Jobs' whole life and work could be summarized definitely as the road less traveled and certainly not centered on *"groupthink."*

Steve Jobs
1955-2011

An example of the keys to his early success was in capturing the entire schoolchildren market with computers when they were only being used in the business sector because of the high cost and lack of software. Steven Jobs actually made the atomic bomb that completely exploded into the entire visual arts and design markets by his just wandering-off and learning everything about typography. Little did he realize at the time that it would be one of the major steps that would launch Apple Inc. as the complete standout in the newly formed computer industry of the mid to late '70s.

> ***"I decided to take a calligraphy class to learn how to [learn calligraphy]. I learned about serif and sans-serif typefaces, about varying the space between different letter combinations, about what makes great typography great. It was beautiful. Historical. Artistically subtle in a way that science can't capture."***
>
> *(– Steve Jobs, Apple Inc. Imagineer)*

I know this firsthand because it is my own experience, even right now as I write this book on my Mac PowerBook with a forty-inch monitor and seamlessly communicate with my iPhone. I know the complete history because it was my history as well. Prior to Apple, there were other European companies emerging that could create logos and typography, in fact, very well. However, if you didn't have millions of dollars and the time to try to assemble these complex systems to find the horsepower and special training to use them, the only reasonable alternative was the laborious cut and pasting of type and all the artistic and graphic design hand tools.

I know all too well because almost fifteen years of my life, I spent doing all of my graphic design by hand and using type sizing math and tools that would take several days and huge amounts of money to complete complex brochures and catalogs. Today on my Mac, I can do it in literally seconds and print it off in full color and present it to my clients via the internet or email for their approval in full color. It is simply a modern-day miracle!

By the time you did this in old school method's with handwritten instructions it was simply horribly laborious and notes and instructions off just to get a few galleys of type finished. The process was massive and very non-creative. First, it was exhausting and secondly, you could blow your complete budget before you were finished with your work because of last-minute client changes or a cup of coffee spilled on your entire day or weeks work. Once you were all done with the design boards for each page with the multiple overlays of instructions and color indications and PMS colors specified with chips you had to tape to the boards, it then went to the client for approval and then corrections where inevitably, so you had to cut in an "e" where they had misspelled with an "o".

The entire design and mechanical process is no still not complete yet, even after several days since you initially started the design process. Next, it would go out for photographing camera with glass plates, converted into film, developed dried, and the stripped on a light table into position with all the sizes and crop marks meticulously made perfect. Make a full-sized proof, have it looked over, and reread for errors, correct any errors, and that was all done.

Well, it was then photographically burned into aluminum plates and put on a giant Heidelberg press, and then each color was spun up and tested and again another color and alignment check of tiny four-color dots. I haven't even told you half of all this nonsense. This process would absolutely make most designers today on their micro-computing devices and smartphones pull their hair out and maybe an arm or two. The good old days really weren't the good old days in the graphic design and printing world ever. Have you had enough yet? Probably so, I have for a lifetime. Now because of the genius of Steve Jobs, you simply scan your photos or drop stock or client photos they sent you on email or off the internet into a simple program like I am using right now called Pages—so simple. Place and drop in the copy the client sent you in a Word program or off the email. Place it in a predesigned and formatted template, tweak the type size and fonts, and save it to PDF. Sent it to the client in only a few minutes or hours. Done! They check it even on shared programs online, and you tweak it in real time and send it to LA or NY or your local FedEx or quick print and it will be digitally printed in full color with 100 percent of the resolution you originally made it in from your final PDF.

So you think that inventing the iPhone is the only achievement of Steve Jobs? No, he completely revolutionized how everyone on the planet now is able to do the highest quality graphics, photography, video, and computing anywhere, anytime. There are no words to describe the wonder the absolute wizardry of this ma n's contributions through Apple.

Les LaMotte working *"Old School"* at his first position as Graphic Designer and part of the Finance Team for InterVarsity Christian Fellowship on Langdon Street in Madison Wisconsin - 1973

*"I was definitely one of those early Apple adopter designers. If it wasn't for Steve Jobs concentrating on the small nuances of typography and eventually revolutionizing the world of graphic design and printing, I would never have taken a second look at the computer world. Everything he touched turned the design world upside down, sending us all at warp speed into a new generation of creativity. Thank you, Steve."*

(*– Les LaMotte • Imagineer, 2018*)

# Great American Imagineers

## Benjamin Franklin, Mechanical & Science Imagineer

Benjamin Franklin, whose rather humble home in Boston that I had a chance to visit, was also a renaissance imagineer of his time. Much like the colorful and broadly adaptive Leonardo da Vinci, he was involved with many areas because he had a capacity to learn, develop, and master each of many disciplines enough to see the convergence of all of them. This is the "key to the Imagineers mind-set and toolbox." He experimented with science, kites, and lightning-producing electricity; he was a guru in his writings and publishing, all of which led him to be a key statesman in forming our nation's most important founding documents The Declaration of Independence and the Constitution which  still governs, and assuring our freedom carrying on what God has empowered our country to do and become. Somewhere along the way, we skipped over the Imagineer approach and began adopting only the highly financed and overly planned approach. Now, I am not mocking anyone who has gone to school and has come out with their MBAs or degrees in business or finance. However, the vast majority of successful entrepreneurs today never went to college or university and spent most of their creative years digging in and finding out how to trade in some form of capitalism, which is merely making, buying, and/or selling of a product or service.

## Thomas Edison, DC Power Imagineer

Thomas Edison is a very good example of one that changed our entire world by giving us the lightbulb. Good thing he wasn't going for the phonograph as he was considered legally deaf.

Everyone proclaims him as a genius; however, he never completed his formal schooling and, in fact, he never got past the eighth grade. I believe because he had other things on his mind. What motivation or core passion did he reveal in his life here when he said, *"I have not heard a bird sing since I was twelve years old."* Despite his major hearing loss, Edison was a renaissance man, much like Leonardo da Vinci. He investigated in his laboratory continuously.

He also was like da Vinci in that he didn't do all the work himself; he hired very good young men that could prove to him that they were worthy of hanging around with him and helping him with his hundreds of inventions.

It is a fact that he even invented the first solar panel over one hundred years ago, and it is still being used in the GE laboratories. Everyone gives him credit for creating the lightbulb; however, he merely found the right combination of filaments to use. That was a miracle in itself as he had tested hundreds of kinds.

## *"I have not heard a bird sing since I was twelve years old ."*

*(–Thomas Edison)*

Some might say that he failed 999 times until *"he eventually found the right one and receive with it the right result."* Failure in life is not an end; it is only the beginning of wisdom that is the ability to stick with something you feel you must fight for. That thing, attitude, service that doesn't work just right, whatever it is in you that creates a need to fix it or build upon it and builds in you the kind of personal character that no matter what life throws at you, you will always land right side up and ten feet tall.

Like an oyster far below the surface of the sea that one day has an uninvited guest of a grain of sand in its fleshy part of its shell. It automatically and immediately takes evasive action by continuously coating it with a crystalline secretion called nacre producing a complete solution of protection for itself to stop the irritation it is experiencing. The result of its evasive work is a beautiful one-of-a-kind round pearl of beauty and of great value to others unlike all other gemstones or precious metals that are refined from the earth.

*"Ask yourself, what is the grain of sand in your life that you and only you were sent here to form into a beautiful and priceless pearl?"*

(– Les LaMotte • *Imagineer*)

## Tesla, AC Power Imagineer

AC Power—no one really talks about this wonder anymore. Why because like everything we just take it for granted. Edison hired Nikola Tesla, who became one of Edison's apprentices with his own completely amazing inventions and would soon overshadow Edison and became his main competition in the race for electricity. Tesla was a true scientific inventor and not a mire marketer and patent holder like Edison who was very full of himself and his accomplishments investing heavily into lawsuits on his hundreds of product patents. Edison, like Steve Jobs, was really more of a marketer than an inventor. He tried to convince the world at that time that the only way to power the lightbulb was to use DC current, probably because it worked for him and he had many patents that would give him control of it. Turns out his proposal was not a real efficient nor cost-effective solution at that time. The only way Edison could create an entire network to service a huge city would require one expensive generating station about every mile. Tesla, tried to convince Edison and his financial backers that his invention of AC or *"alternating current"* was much safer than DC current and didn't require frequent generating stations and could serve a larger customer base from longer distances from where the current was being used. Therefore, it was the best price and delivery for electrical current for the investors. Guess who won? Tesla, of course, and for the last one hundred years in the United States and around the world, AC has been the die-hard standard current.

## Imagineering Continues

Everyone has heard or seen solar panels in use today, and they seem to be seen just everywhere, an extremely and growing alternative to a renewable power source that can be powered from anywhere without exterior wires or AC current. So how did we go from everyone demanding AC power to most people, especially in Germany and California where it is now required on every house in the next few years. It's easy; we don't need power from stations a long way away any longer. We can now receive the power from our roofs or backyard solar farms. So the entire picture in one hundred years has turned around one hundred and eighty degrees, and if Thomas Edison were alive today and still working on solar solutions, he would have won over Tesla with DC power, another Imagineer ahead of his time. Today, as AC begins to fade away in the overwhelming acceptance and cost advantages of DC power and its portable aspect in cars and trucks and ubiquitous in all electronics, the continued use of AC is forcing us to use little black *"wall warts"* inverters or adding weight and cost to our digital devices to convert the AC we make to DC, which all electronics run on. The deception is that while they are using AC, we are losing 25 percent of the electricity in the process of conversion to DC so they can operate correctly. What a waste of electricity and our money. Our huge advances in wind power, which was thought to be the answer and billions of public dollars of investment, has proven to be a total miscalculation and another big business scam.

Solar Panel Installation on a House Roof.

They raised the money within the power companies from us and then sold off the assets and made money on our investment of purchasing the equipment. Then only to find out that they are only producing less than a few percent of our energy needs. However, PR and a lot of nice pictures of and stories on wind power success can camouflage any of the low-thinking *"leave me alone, I want to watch my ball game"* mentality that makes up the vast majority of today's society we have become.

Thermal power is being looked at and it is still in the beginning stages, but there are some bright hopes for it as well in the future. Continuing to produce only AC power is no longer really a good concept for the consumer today; it seems only good for large-scale power plants to keep the costs of energy higher and higher. It seems that we as a nation and society are a bit schizophrenic about how we make decisions on large changes in power, and it appears to be more politically motivated rather then practically innovative or what is best for the consumer. Power demand around the world just keeps getting larger and larger. We have been fooled into thinking in the early fifties and sixties that nuclear was the only answer, but in the last few years, the cost and danger of having to isolate populations from the unspent nuclear fuel rods has reached alarming expense and resistance to any state to actually put it in the ground for safekeeping, as if there really was any. Even in places like Africa, the need for reliable power uses the same political motivations by continuing to propose large power plants that are not sustainable based on the low incomes there because of the pressure from the United States and European power

Wind Energy up close with the working generator which is the size of an 18 wheel trailer and blades over 100' long.

companies, instead of putting in place the obvious lower-cost investment in solar and wind for the local village power supplies and larger solar and wind farms for major cities.

I know from being on three trips to East Africa that it is not the will of the people that they do not have good infrastructure and power, but the political nature of the leaders who choose to keep the money they receive for themselves rather than build the needed infrastructure to provide even the most basic of services to their people. They have failed in harnessing the real power they already have, and that is the education and creative ability of their people. If the local villagers were given solar education and knowledge of how to build it and use it, it would completely begin to be used everywhere. The people would begin to own the technologies and provide for themselves through self-empowerment.

When I was in Washington DC, I sat next to a man from NASA who was responsible for engineering the moon landings, who stated that the country of South Sudan has one of the largest potentials for making solar energy in the entire world. The natural resources of Africa is enormous and easily available. Solar and wind technology could completely change the future advances in education, manufacturing, and stabilization of all the African continent's economics.

Les LaMotte developed a plan to teach the making of Solar panels and Solar chargers throughout Africa as SolarTrek™ International.



This is the very thing that we seek to do around the world in third world and emerging countries. We have plans to begin to empower people in with these very things to improve their lives, by training individuals in Solar power, and teaching them how to build it, store it, and use it. Visit my subside at LesLaMotte.com and support our plans for future Solar Education and development.

## Imagineers Flying Like an Eagle

The other large enterprise that was launched and took off in record speed in the sixties was *"NASA,"* which took imagineering to a whole new level of science and technology.

So as we progress, we also repeat history as in the case of the recent works by Elon Musk, who has amassed several companies that on the outside don't seem connected—electric cars, SpaceX, and batteries. Well, I guess the first and the last are very much related. However, even the name Tesla on his cars harkens back to the long-standing duo and struggle of Edison and Tesla (the man). However, in this case, the new Tesla car is fighting for a place in the history of reengineering and imagineering as it is using DC power, which they have planned to make available via solar power as they progress and large battery storage for homes to charge their electric cars and the cars to power the houses. Isn't that an interesting twist of fate, or is it just how history always comes back with using similar concepts and technologies only in new and entirely different ways?

So the concept of Imagineering or being an Imagineer was born like products out of *need and desire* to accomplish something you couldn't pull off the shelf.

The individual Imagineer explores many and various technologies and finds connections and similarities that no one else has ever identified. Once identified, they can research and develop products that can in many cases launch entirely new concepts that have never been tried or tested before. They simply had to be designed, engineered, and tested while always looking for ways to improve on techniques, costs, results, and performance, and most of all, their effectiveness in relation to the people who first choose to be adaptors to inspire the rest of humanity who are too cautious to allow rapid change. Change is inevitable, and no one likes change because

it runs counter to our humanity and inner core that is always trying to find peace and tranquility.

That too hasn't changed; it is still the same as all business is business, in the end even for the Imagineer. His far-out ideas must find some landing place in order for the general public to engage their new concepts. This process takes time, and this is where the Imagineer must morph into the marketer such as Steve Jobs or simply remain an inventor like Tesla, who although he created enormous amounts of patents and products, almost 90 percent of them are still either not understood or never found their way to the general market. When Tesla died in his apartment in New York, all of his patents and designs were snatched up by some say the US government and never seen again.

Even an Imagineer like Elon Musk has quickly encountered some difficulties and debilitation that comes from initiating the development of large organizations.

They can begin with a tremendous explosion of creativity and end up with tons of deadweight in the middle between those who really get their hands dirty in getting the job done and those who end up only pushing paper around and going to meetings. Another case of *"more don't make better."* Or committees in general are totally void of design that is anything earthshaking because of the basis of who and what they are and how they function as they are a committee. Members are there because they were chosen, and the human dynamics over time gives a cushion to or eliminates the *"risk-taking creative activities"* of the founders and original Imagineers.

**"I learned a significant technique of communication and enacting change at Skyline Displays® in the late 80's. The corporate culture included all employees to stand while conducting corporate meetings ensuring that they were short, to the point and done extremely quickly saving**

*tons of corporate employee time in confusion. It also translates to building disciple and an urgency to show up on time, puts the important news on the top mind of everyone who move directly to implementing the changes throughout the entire company seamlessly and simultaneously."*

*(– Les LaMotte • Imagineer)*

Committees can only make decisions that end-up as something that everyone can agree with; therefore, the end results can only be the *lowest common denomination.* The boards' main purpose is to simply keep the investors' money safe and secure rather then creating the next best thing. Therefore, just like Apple when Steven Jobs was tossed out of his company because he wasn't doing a good enough job of keeping the budgets in line with investors' requirements. Instead, they brought in an accountant type to watch over the money until the Apple cow ran out of milk for lack of new and original ideas and constant updates. They eventually lost huge chunks of market share in this development defunding and delaying process, until they brought Steve Jobs back who then single handedly created the greatest boon to Apples stock no one could imagine—the iPad and the iPhone, and ultimately changing the entire worlds communications and social structure forever.

Lt Colonel Joshua LaMotte and three of my oldest grandchild at the Burnsville Fire Muster Parade in our New Zealand Blo-Cart®.

> ## *"A lot of middle-managers adding costs but not doing anything obviously useful ."*
>
> ### *(– Elon Musk)*

Quote by Manish Dudharejia, guest writer, founder, and president of E2M Solutions Inc., July 25, 2018, article "Elon Musk's 'Productivity' Email to Tesla Employees Is Required Reading for Every Entrepreneur," Entrepreneur online magazine.

# Has the Role of the Entrepreneur Been Hijacked?

## Is Getting Your MBA The Only Way

Contrary to the highly educated elite class of today, who believe that in order to do something right or really important, you must spend huge amounts of money and have fancy and flashy degrees from the right prestigious school such as Harvard, Yale, or Stanford or any other kind of institution of *"distinctive higher learning"*. The original entrepreneurs by necessity went out and found something they could do, liked, and perfected it. They had to figure out on their own how to grow it, or they bought it from another successful entrepreneur at a fair price. They built a company they could make enough revenue that was more than their expenses and managed to make a small profit for it to continue year after year.

## Kind of Makes Sense, Doesn't It?

Downright simple to understand, nothing fancy or sophisticated about it. Work hard at producing the best they could and build a lasting reputation for a great business that was enjoyed by all. These same entrepreneurs, because of their thankfulness, went out into the community and used the wealth they had been given to help their community and its people. Possibly because of their faith in God or kindness in their hearts, they decided to do something to help others and picked up a hammer and helped to paint, repair, or build homes in their community.

Today, those kind of people, who have the ability to see the position of wealth as having been entrusted to them to be a servant to others, are hard to find.

However, it is not that they never existed, but rather there are few who teach these qualities of self-improvement for the good of others. In fact, they see business entrepreneurs as having the financial blessings of God so that they had enough to overflow and share with others with consistent acts of kindness and action where there weren't any. They even took their wealth and didn't distinguish between different skin colors, kinds, religions, and languages, eventually expanding their reach all around the world.

## Imagineers with Dreams for Homes

I had the distinct honor and privilege to sit down with just such a man at a busy trade show here in Minneapolis a few years ago. He was a real honest-to-goodness modern hero and larger-than-life legend. He asked me to sit down and have lunch with him and offered me half of his peanut butter sandwich. While we were sitting there, our hearts grew very familiar, and we became instant friends. I felt a certain distinction of being ministered to by a real servant of God. His eyes were intense, yet filled with humility and just the way he was some fifty years earlier. As a young attorney when he closed his successful attorney's office and packed up his family along with his hard-earned million dollars from his savings account. I suddenly felt a distinct honor to be in his presence and having shared that ordinary peanut butter sandwich with him and hearing firsthand in a few moments as he imparted to me his heart and his calling from God. Just speaking to him encouraged and strengthened my heart as to what it means for a person to have a dream and the firm commitment to seeing their dream fulfilled despite the encumbrance or loss of status and position in life.

After our unique heart-to-heart lunch, still feel the warmth of his genuine spirit as he shared with me that day. However, only a few weeks later, I was terribly saddened that in those few short weeks, he passed from this earth to his heavenly home that Jesus had built for him. Isn't that simply amazing? He spent his entire life here on earth building homes for others. I am quite sure he knew in his heart that Jesus was building one for him for eternity. His special gift to countless hundreds of thousands of people and communities that have been lifted up

and given a new life by his simple, but profound sacrifice of his selfless giving to others. Do you think he truly understood his purpose in life? I do and I know that many today are living lives that are also filled by this one ma n's sacrificial giving to their families, neighbors, and communities.

*"From the one who has been entrusted with much, much more will be asked."*
*(– Luke 12:48, KJ)*

Yes, that special and inspiring moment I shared was with none other than the Habitat for Humanity founder, Millard Fuller. You may have never heard of Millard before, but you certainly know of his dream. He was so humble that for the sake of the work he was given, he simply allowed it to be wrapped with other more well-known personalities that you know extremely well. Maybe you even believed that they, not Millard, refused to take center stage so that their celebrity could be used to bring greater influence and focus of the fund-raising, such as President Jimmy Carter.

*"Habitat for Humanity is a perfect example of the Power of Capitalism to enhance the Spirit of America and its concern for all of its people. It is simply Business at its finest with a careful balance of Power and Strength focused and committed to one common goal that the deal maker, must also be the change maker because of their profit and to use it in the lives of their community. Thank you, Millard Fuller, Habitat for Humanity Founder, for your wonderful and fruitful example of a lifelong hard-fought legacy of being the Imagineer uniting us to 'Make America Great Again!' I know that President Donald Trump would totally agree with your contributions."*
*(– Les LaMotte • Imagineer, 2019)*

**12**



## Innovation for Results®

### The Next Shinny Object

Most of the business world today are busy looking for the next new thing or product or service, and they need to because that is just what they have been programmed by their customers to think about, or the opposite is true—the customers are preprogrammed and wired in their DNA to always search for the next new thing and especially if it is on SALE in the Minnesota mind-set.

> *"Entrepreneurship is neither a science nor an art. It is a practice."*
>
> *(– Peter Drucker)*

1997 – Son Jordan (President), Les, (CEO) and Son Lt Colonel Joshua LaMotte - building some of the first Xtra Lite Displays in Les's basement design studio. Working on our custom designed duel work benches. Complete with drill and soft model tire to insert the shock cord automatically in to the sequence of poles.

When I was first starting out in the design world, now almost five centuries ago, the ones to beat were the Europeans. It seemed that they were the only ones getting it right with extremely highly designed brands you would instantly recognize, such as very fine jewelry, clothing, and wine/beer. We as Americans were simply mesmerized about how they could achieve such high standards and PR-covered mystique and make the products with such craftsmanship. The truth about their high quality and their high prices to boot were that they were all manufactured in small cottage industries. Sound familiar? Yes, it is exactly how we started by bringing that same concept to America by the European settlers. This cottage industry, although needed people working together and hight coordinated, it still maintained an extremely high quality and price, it was for a while also hard to find in

America; and that too was a key to their success in getting the high price they desired. The key to these cottage industries was that the people who did the work weren't paid by the hour; they were paid by the job or by the parts they made, much of which was still made by hand in small shops across Europe or wine from small regions of family-owned farms in France, Italy and slavic countries.

The advantage of this form of manufacturing was that people actually had to deliver, and if they didn't, they didn't receive any payment. This very fact helped keep the high-quality standards in place there. The individuals would go to the master company brands and receive their orders for manufacturing and pick up the parts and return them at a certain time requested when completed. If they didn't match the expected standards and quality of the brand company, they were not paid as much or not at all.

This kind of self-discipline forced them to either do it extremely well or not bother doing it at all. It also allowed them to live the live style they enjoyed and they managed to maintained a personal pride in their work and were richly rewarded for the quality they could provide.

However, after many years, products began to need to be competitive, and so the greedy businesses moved away from the locally hand-produced products to machine-made goods and eventually to overseas or places in East Asia to be manufactured in which they had varying standards of quality.

At the same time, because in the United States we grew so fast, our products had to be made in large labor sweatshops from which Europe would use to manufacture their linens and cotton products. As Americans, we passed right over the handmade high quality to high volume by necessity, and we lost the high quality standards and systems that the Europeans were able to hang on to much longer. The result was that people who were wealthy in the US and around the world and continued their love affair with Europe's high quality that they had grown accustomed to and continued to by the illusion of European hight quality products.

1999 – Tokyo Japan, Les seeing for the first time the Xtra Lite Displays used to greet everyone that came off the planes coming into Japan.



12

Many in Europe still harbor a disdain for American-made goods especially the elite class who believe that our goods lack craftsmanship, design, and quality even today.

### *"The best time to plant a tree was 20 years ago. The second best time is now."*
*(– Chinese proverb)*

Today, however, most of the products that were made in Europe have gone the same route as those in the United States, and we both make our products in East Asia where the prices have been more affordable for many years.

I went to Disney in Orlando directly myself, however, they didn't purchase the Xtra Lite until they saw my product in a trade show in Tokyo, Japan.

This single exhibit in Tokyo Japan in 1999 was the reason we won Walt Disney, Universal Studios, and Travel South USA.

With the advent of new tighter regulations on tariffs by President Trump, who has worked hard at reversing that tendency of thought, the United States is beginning to once more prefer goods made in the United States.

When I visited South Korea, who used to make all the Nike shoes with huge factories that I saw in Seoul, these large global brands even then were all gone. The economic conditions have risen so high that even the Koreans are now manufacturing in China. Now, the factories in South Korea are importing people from Southeast Asia and importing lower-priced workers from Vietnam and Bangladesh.

### *"When everything seems to be going against you, remember that the airplane takes off against the wind, not with it."*
*(– **Henry Ford,** founder of Ford Motor Company)*

### *"It's not about ideas. It's about making ideas happen."*
*(– **Scott Belsky**, co-founder of Behance)*

What is the very thing in life that you experience or hear about on a daily basis that just drives you crazy because in your estimation it is NOT done correctly or is missing altogether? You believe that you have a unique way to solve this challenge to make this world a better place or an easier place to live. You believe you have been placed here because you have the unique gifts and talents to make it right! There you are, I just handed over to you a million-dollar idea that you have been carrying around with you for maybe sometime.

The only thing you lacked is approval by someone like myself who has broken through the "glass ceiling" of our own bubble that keeps us in the prison of our own minds. So why are you reading this? Get going, you have a mission to complete!

> **"To any entrepreneur: If you want to do it, do it now. If you don't, you're going to regret it."**
> *(– Catherine Cook, cofounder of MyYearbook)*

*"Even as the CEO of my own company it took every ounce of my confidence in my Xtra Lite Display products to realize I would be presenting it to one of the largest entertainment companies in the world!"*

1998 - one year after my start-up Universal Studios Orlando became one of my largest clients by volume of displays purchased.

## Misconceptions of What it Takes to Be in Business

**Take an Informed Look…**

*Les's Rule #1 of Thumb: The contents of your wallet is NOT your Steering Wheel!*

## You don't need a lot of money.

Rich people invest in other people's hard work. Entrepreneurs build things, and things can be services as well as products. They start very often with little or no money. Your financial success is out of reach as long as you're delaying acting on your success plan due to increasing your bank balance. Forget cash and think opportunity.

*Les's Rule #2 of Thumb: You don't need to be a CPA or an MBA… you can hire them! You don't need a business education.*

## You don't need a business education.

The next time you go into the bank to conduct a transaction at a teller window, you're probably looking at a college graduate with a business degree. Where did all that education get them? We're not belittling them, just pointing out that years of business courses do not make a successful entrepreneur. Whatever you know, you know enough if you have the desire to make it happen. Besides, you can learn or hire the business basics to get a successful start.

*Les's Rule #3 of Thumb: You only need to serve your customers providing that unique thing or service they are looking for!*

## You don't need a unique idea or to invent something.

Sure, if you come up with something better than Velcro® or a whole new food group for a fast-food franchise, you're going to be rich. But the new product or service idea isn't necessary to start a business. You could simply have a desire to make a better product or provide a better service but simply meet people needs.

*Les's Rule #4 of Thumb: You don't have to quit your job and go out to borrow tons of money before you begin.*

## You don't need to start big or quit your day job.

A large percentage of successful entrepreneurs started their businesses part-time from their homes. They continued to work at their jobs to fund their lifestyles while they invested mostly time and effort in their new businesses.

*"The critical ingredient is getting off your butt and doing something. It's as simple as that. A lot of people have ideas, but there are few who decide to do something about them now. Not tomorrow. Not next week. But today. The true entrepreneur is a doer, not a dreamer."*

*(– Nolan Bushnell, Entrepreneur)*

# My Passion for Xtra Lite Displays®

## The Dorris Connection

Actually, it didn't start in Nashville or even in Minneapolis, but in Jakarta, Indonesia. What? How did that thread happen? At the time, I had spent five years working for one of the best-known designers for Unilever products. Dorris called me one day while I was sitting in the design office in my basement at that time. She said that she had found my name in a designer's reference book that no one had ever called me from in twenty-two years. She was coming to Minneapolis from New York City and wanted to interview me for working with her on packaging design. Having really no idea of who she was, what she had done, I, of course, said, *"Yes, please come, I will meet with you."* So in a week, she arrived. I was a bit shocked as she really looked like and smelled like she was from New York in her very beautiful designer clothing, smelling of a very fine perfume that wafted throughout our house every time she came. I was kind of embarrassed at first as my wife did daycare upstairs and I had my design office in our basement.

Doris's eyes grew rather large as she noticed all children and came down to see my office / design studio, but then she said she liked children.

I was getting kind of worried as I was not dressed as high styled as she was and certainly my little humble design office was nothing fancy. So we sat at my round

I worked as Packaging Designer for Dorris du Cret Design Group – An Award - Winning International Packaging Design Firm.

glass table, and I showed her my work. She seemed kind of impressed. However, she then brought out her work, and I was totally blown away! Every brand I ever knew including 7-Eleven was in her portfolio. Wow, was all I could say. We sat and talked and then she said, *"Let's begin tomorrow."*

So that began our relationship for the next five years of designing bottles, logotypes, and product packaging for many worldwide brands all over Southeast Asia because that is where she continued to win the contracts every year when she visited their offices in London. The work we did together won the contracts from one of the most prestigious design firms in London at the time. This wonderful relationship and work continued for five years, and then it was announced that the Asian Tiger had collapsed. After that, Dorris lost her contracts in Indonesia, Australia, New Zealand, China, Philippines, and Mexico. Because Unilever moved from designing each brand in each country to designing one brand in every country, therefore, the need for our packaging design ended.

There were many years where Doris asked me what the bill for the next year would be and then hand me a check for hundreds of thousands of dollars before the year began. She was an excellent client to have, and she became an extremely good friend.

## Get Ready for the Next Opportunity

How did I get from working as a graphic/packaging designer to beginning a record label and going to the GMA Week in Nashville? My thread connection was my work in the prisons, and the result was recording and designing my own CD in 1994, *"Sonrise A New Tomorrow"*, containing nine of my original songs.

After producing "Sonrise A New Tomorrow" of 9 original songs, I pursued designing and producing CDs for other artists. So where better to find other Christian artists in need of marketing and design than at the GMA *(Gospel Music Association)* Week in Nashville?

## Seize the Opportunity

I was always a tinkerer; I played with products, tested them, tried them, tore them apart to see how they worked. I found out that new ideas and the pure imagineering process does not come from a committee. It comes from individuals who see what others cannot see. Like Michelangelo who didn't carve a statue, he saw a work of art in the stone, and *"he was only chipping away the rock to release it to the world."*

**14**

*My Passion for Xtra Lite Displays®*

"The Atlas" by Michelangelo 1530

## Nashville or Bust!

After having recorded my first CD album "*Sonrise A New Tomorrow*" and doing the jacket and insert designs for it, I realized that my work with Dorris in packaging had come to an

abrupt end. I found myself out of packaging design work, and much of my other design work had dwindled during my five years of working with Dorris because of her demand for the majority of work for her.

I decided that after having been in graphic design for almost thirty years and because of our prison music work, I decided to take a musical diversion; maybe it was time to explore a new avenue and exhibit at the Nashville GMA *(Gospel Music Association)* Week on April 21, 1994, *(my wedding anniversary—sorry, dear)*. Shortly after, I finished up my own album and CD design and possibly pick up some of the Christian artists' CD and marketing design work. So my very good friend Peter, who is an extraordinary marketing genius and good brother in Christ, we had our separate companies, mine graphic design and packaging and his marketing and writing books; and we worked together on many corporate projects, such as the Scotch Audio & Video Tape Division of 3M. Sorry, for all those who have never used a recording tape; it was machine that used always get wound up wrong and, well, you know what I mean—the stuff your parents used, they were a pain in the neck. Sit down and thank Steven Jobs for a better option.

So we designed and created a display for the GMA show that would work for both of our businesses. Since one of our mutual clients at the time was a company in Minneapolis that was sewing banners, we decided to have them make the banners for us.

Digital graphics was just finding its legs and still was very expensive and hard-to-find outlets for large scale printing. Prior to going to the show, I had been getting requests from another show I attended in Houston for singers and songwriters. While I was down there, I also did some musical prison ministry, which I will talk about in another chapter.

So we packed up my old Chevy with all of my metal and banner displays and plastic display podium and CD racks I had made by another plastics client I was working with. Believe me, we had everything we could do to squeeze it all into my small car. Another little wrinkle was that because we were going to be traveling so far to Nashville the day before, I had my brakes all redone so they would be ready for the long trip.

## We Set Off for Nashville

We were traveling along without a hitch and were in southern Indiana when we noticed that the car was not running quite the same and presenting a little drag. By the time we reached Nashville and pulled to a stoplight on our way to find some dinner, we looked back to see smoke and flames coming out of our back wheels. I jumped out of the car and ran to see what was going on, and it looked like we were going to have barbecued tires for supper. We had no idea what had happened, and having all this stuff in the car and the possibility that it was all going to go up in smoke was totally frightening. We quickly pulled over off the road to see what we could do. It was then we realized that

we no longer had any brakes. We somehow were able to push the car down the street to a local brake repair company on the other side of the road, thank you Lord! it was only about a block away. They told us the bad news that our brakes had ceased and that they would have to be totally done over. To a guy who wasn't all that fat with cash, especially since I just paid for it the day before at home and was hoping to make something at the show, it was totally overwhelming to hear that it would cost another five hundred dollars to redo the brakes. We had no choice and asked them if they could do it right away, and they said they would. We both breathed a sigh of relief and bit the bullet to get it done one more time.



14

*My Passion for Xtra Lite Displays®*

So late that night, we made it to the Nashville convention hall and inquired as to where our exhibit was and then made our way through the long hallways through the back drive-in alley. These cheap heavy metal banner stands were so heavy and cumbersome that when I thought about using them again, I asked myself why in the world did I think this was going to be easy to pull off.

So we sweated through it and finally got all the gear to the exhibit hall. We were so tired we just left it there and went out to find a place for the night. The next day, we set it all up before the show started, and boy, did it take a long and tedious time! But we managed to get it done just as the show opened.
Sometime during the show, a man with cameras hanging from around his neck by the name of Scott came by our booth and said he really liked our exhibit design and wanted to know if we could make one like this for him, only of much lighter weight and portable.

## The Art, Science, and Math behind the Display Structure

I realized as I looked at the heavy banner stands we were using and realized that they weren't that far from a tent. It had four connection corners, with the poles arched and connected together the first time with some wires and a hole. I realized that it was simply a tent standing on its side, and the floor was the graphic. I had not designed something absolutely original; I had absolutely innovated a technology-like tents that could now support graphics and banners. It was so simple; why hadn't anyone else thought of it before?
It just goes to show you that the ***"NEED is the SEED"*** of Invention. I learned early on in my training in graphic design that describing the challenge and all the limitations that the answer to the problem or challenge was within the definition. If you simply outline all aspects of the challenge and can turn them into words, the answer will come popping out at you. For the words are the necessary research within the challenge.

*(© 2019 – Les LaMotte · Imagineer.)*

The basic modern tent had been engineered many years prior in the early '50s. The need continued in the race for space and to make lightweight systems for extending and holding the early lightweight compact and delicate solar panels in space.
I discovered that I had been studying the geodesic dome and how the overall skin tension was a necessary part of the stress that would hold the dome together, the same with the work that Orville and Wilbur Wright had to engineer into their first airfoil wings of their glider/plane so it could be lightweight and strong. They used cables in $X$ patterns that would cause the stress to unite and strengthen the entire structure. Buildings and bridges have the same kind of stress applied to cables running through the inside of them to secure them in place with the fluctuation of the wind forces on skyscrapers and towers.

I just borrowed the same principles in my design and placed the $X$ at the back, transferring the tension of the back $X$ structure through an imaginary $X$ to the front of the fabric or graphic so the tension would be equally distributed, allowing it to stand straight and tall. I then added a pole straight down the back that was held in a right triangular angle to the opposing $X$ forces, causing the banner to stand upright. The tents didn't have the need of this vertical connection part, and it was a critical stabilization element to make it a self-standing tension structure.

I then realized that what was to become the Xtra Lite Display was a combination of all that I ever learned about kites, Boy Scouts and tenting, and graphics. These were the three keys to my success. It wasn't simply my design drawings or whimsical concepts, but that I had employed the very root of every structure to that of triangulation. These same principles of triangulation are the basis of the geodesic dome. All of this kind of thinking is Imagineering at its best and why the study of many converging principles and technologies are important. The universe is created from the interplay and connection of billions of these same structural concept components on a nanoscale that are not seen by the

I visited the Epson headquarters in downtown Tokyo. The entire showroom of their printing products was being displayed using Xtra Lite Displays XL1. That was a delight to see something you made in your basement being used to display one of the worlds largest corporations products not even in your country, but, in Japan.

naked eye and, therefore, highly overlooked by most people. It is all in our Creator God's enormous and wonderful design, proving to me further we are not here by chance but by intentional design to the very core.

I continued for a few minutes to just look at the structure and how perfectly it worked. I had built this highly sophisticated structure in my basement with nothing but my mind, a graphic design background, observations as a Scout, and my prior knowledge of the new wave that was about to hit of digital printing in the late 80's. There were 3D graphics at the time but highly restricted in price of the software and the huge learning curve to be effective with it. I know as I had tried using some only a few years prior in packaging design, and I found it at that time extremely hard to master.

Rather, I designed my bottles by slicing them up into equal horizontal segments from bottom to top, measured the width from the center, and entered in the raw data into a spreadsheet to determine the volume of the bottle. Then as I changed the design of the outer shape of the bottle, I would redo the sizes and discover its new volume. Very slow, but very exacting process, which today is easily calculated by 3D computer programs, and it automatically updates the volume based on the shape as you change the overall design by simply pulling it into a new shape. Somehow, I was able to use simple *"golden proportions"* theory of visual and structural proportional perfection used to design the structure in drawings or painting, giving the exact proportions to make amazingly balanced compositions and use of space.

These exacting proportions were the key to determining the size you wanted to make an Xtra Lite Display no matter how high or how wide. But it wasn't that easy. My son Josh, who just graduated from college and on his way to beginning his army career, was familiar with some of the early database programs. I challenged him to help me build the right system in which the computer could do the calculations to get us this same golden-proportioned display no matter what size we were looking to make. Josh went right to work and began using his math background and utilized the quadratic formula to determine the hypotenuse of the right triangle, and we eventually determined that adding an inch to the back standard pole was the perfect formula to get it to stand up with enough slack to match my original system geometry.

As you changed display sizes, the formula and sequence of the use of variable sizes of tubing, plus the need to know the length of the return tube sequence so that the *"fid"* or reduced size of the insert tube was in the right place and side of the tubing, we would cut off the right sizes and deburr the tubing rather than cut off the fid, which needed to be flipped around to secure the tubing leg. This we learned by carefully uncovering the exact knotting sequence and bungee cord termination techniques. Once they were found, Josh's formula would give us all the right dimensions so we could directly have the drawings to build any sized the custom-sized product. This customizing on the fly was one of our best attributes and selling points of our product, and no one else offered it and it became a distinguishing element of our overall success.

The other physical characteristics that required changes included the sequence of how it would fold up to make the tightest package for use. These variables had to be preprogrammed into the actual leg length and the height of the back support leg as well as the size of the bottom-right triangle, and whether one or more parts that were needed to form the bottom-right triangle. All of these factors had to be considered and adjusted according to the size of the display to be made. With all of these changeable variables, he accomplish this to perfection with the XL1 calculator no matter what the size we wanted to build. His calculator did these calculations and not only the numbers but it also produced a printable graphical planning chart that the builder could visually and reliably follow. He was able to figure out the right cuts by using a series of logic *"if this, then"* mathematical statements so it would give us the right cuts, making the best and most economical use of the aluminum tubing at the same time.



*My Passion for Xtra Lite Displays®*

**14**

The entire project took about three months, and we finally had a program that would not only give us the proportions but also how to make it the most efficient and cost-effective way. This became a real time-saver and gave consistency to every display no matter what the size was. It was the *"custom calculator"* that we needed to really get going fast and with a standard acceptable and assured result.

After we had solved getting the calculator together, I realized that if we could get each size, then why not also figure the base price? So I asked him for one more level of automation in the calculator, which was to add up the cost of all the parts and give us a sum total of the cost of the display so we could easily price it out based on real cost numbers. He finally completed it before he shipped out to South Korea to his first overseas station. Of course, there were small tweaks here and there over the next few years and especially as we needed to adapt it to making some of the other twenty-four kinds of displays, each with their own engineering and golden proportional requirements and challenges built in.

## Threading the Concepts Together

After my many years in the Boy Scouts and having received my Eagle Scout award now fifty years ago as I write this, I was very familiar with working with tents, which ours at the time were made of heavy canvas, much like those used in the Second World War, with heavy wooden poles.

The photo I took for one of my Artists *"Betty"* a very famous Brazilian Gospel Artist that ended up building my business by attracting worldwide attention. This was my $14.00 investment that brought me $14 million in revenue in 14 years.

They were too heavy for anything but putting in a car, not even close to the miniature and lightweight level that was developed by Moss in the mid-fifties as they were focused on the mountaineering and camping industry. Moss remains a well-known name in tenting, and we found them as many years later begin to make displays over the years. While at the Skyline Displays®, I had heard of them but didn't realize the significance of how their invention and my innovation of their design would affect my immediate future with my Xtra Lite Displays® brand.

## My First Solid Approval of Concept

What I had made that day was still a prototype with many extra holes and surface blemishes and small mistakes and so I made a few more additional generations of it through additional emerging prototype refinements.

I learned that if I thought it looked good, it was good, but the real test was if I showed it to someone else like my brother Al, who also was a Boy Scout and experienced in aluminum pole tenting. What would his reaction be?

He dropped over to my house and took a long look at it, and he was speechless for a few moments as he observed just what it was about then broke into an absolute smile of wonder as he was so impressed with this first initial prototype. It instantly spoke to his marketing mind of all the possibilities. He exclaimed to be on the spot that

> ### *"You have to make and market this infant new display product because it is too ingenious and absolutely in demand by the industry."*

(– Dr. Al LaMotte - my confidant and brother.)

I definitely thanked him for his enthusiasm, and this was only the beginning of support I received from my little brother Al, and as a doctor he is definitely smarter than I. Now I had a product, but where would I get enough aluminum poles to begin making it in mass quantities? So I tried to purchase some more initial stock at REI, but unfortunately, I had bought them all out.

## In Search of Poles

As the world of camping progressed since I was an Eagle Scout, the newest and lightest-weight tents began using nylon and getting smaller and smaller, but using stronger aluminum tent pole materials that were bound together with a bungee cord down the center, they quickly self-assembled and you could put them up fast and take them down and fold up the poles in seconds without working with each pole section separately. Very efficient and secure in tight little bundles.

My next question was where could I find tent poles of the highest tension rate and strength? Remember in 1996 a few years before

the internet was ready for prime time you couldn't just search Google or look up on Amazon for these things. The concept of the "warehouse" store hadn't fully been quite created just yet. Then I remembered the REI mountaineering and camping gear store in Bloomington, Minnesota. I always frequented it because of the cool stuff they had. I knew I would never really purchase anything because they were super expensive, but it was the source of some of the very visually stimulating ideas and colors. The look and feel of anodized aluminum always made me want to observe its marvel, and the parts were so aesthetically pleasing to my eye and even better to the touch.

To my joy, you could buy single replacement pole sections one at a time there like the old-time hardware stores. REI had a whole array of poles to choose from and many for only a dollar or two apiece. I purchased as many as they had in stock, just enough to make an initial prototype. I know they also had thin black bungee cord and even small push-in-end tips so I grabbed a handful of the various kinds and twenty-five yards of  bungee and rushed home.

I began by taking my initial drawing idea and immediately began laying out the pieces of tubing and experimenting with just how to cobble the poles and parts together. So I started and it seemed very simple; however, getting the bungee through the pole was extremely hard to do and very slow. I would have to deal with that at a later time and tackle it with perhaps my son Jordan's help. After finishing the structure, I applied the former cloth banner onto it, and I was amazed as to how easy and completely steady it was. As far as I was concerned, it hit it out of the park, being extremely lightweight and rather structurally sound.

The first realization I had was to ask myself, how would I produce large numbers of pole sets if I had to hand feed and thread them through each pole one at a time? After trying a few techniques, I realized that a rubber tire from an outdoor radio-controlled car would work great! So I went down to the local hobby store and purchased a hub assembly and a few four-inch rubber tires and took my electric drill and tried to shoot the bungy cord through all the poles and once. After a few tries and working out a feeding tube from the fid part of the actual tubing, it worked like a charm—and after fourteen years and hundreds of thousands of displays, we used the same mechanism that Jordan and I made on my little workbench in our basement together on a Saturday afternoon. Some further innovations were that of a stand that applied the weight of the drill and allowed it to float on top of the bungee cord, giving it enough grip to shoot it through up to eight feet in one fast shot. I found out later that none of the companies making tent poles was even using this fast and ingenious method.

## Finding the Source

Now I had a product, but where would I get enough aluminum poles to begin making it in mass quantities? So I purchased some more initial stock at REI, but unfortunately, I had bought them all out. I inquired at the local REI as to where there purchasing was done and I found out quickly where their main offices were. They turn out to be in Seattle, Washington. That figures because there are mountains there, and out of necessity comes invention and innovation. As a Minnesotan where we have lakes but no mountains, I was awakened to the knowledge that everyone in the west was climbing mountains and needing lightweight equipment to bring with them.

I quickly called REI and asked for someone who could point me to the one in charge of purchasing their aluminum poles. Well, at first, they were rather reluctant and so I tried to ease their pain by telling them that I was designing a product that was not in direct competition with anything they made. I guess that did the trick, and I got to speak with their buyer. He told me that there were many sources, but they were mostly in Salt Lake City, Utah, in the United States and several others in South Korea. So Salt Lake sounded easy enough so I called Easton and inquired if I could come out and meet with them and share my product and what my needs were for aluminum tubing for my product.

We got our selves into some Chicken Soup with Jack Canteld's Book Promotions for several of his Authors.

I am glad I took the time to learn about the tubing to achieve more intimacy providing greater detail and understanding for me to write into my upcoming marketing and advertising materials allowing me to write with authenticity and knowledge to share with potential buyers.

I was mostly interested in finding out just how these aluminum poles were made and approximately how much they were going to cost and how long it took to get orders filled or if they would even sell them to me at all. I flew out to Salt Lake, and we talked and I saw the process. It was mind-blowing at first with all the machines and huge stacks of aluminum poles. They must have been ten feet long and about one inch in circumference. They took me through all the many steps it took to make these thin little poles that were extremely strong and durable tent poles. I found out that they make the most of them for arrows and that they were the largest manufacturer of arrows in the United States and in many arts of the world. You probably recognize their name from their distinctive aluminum "ping" from their Easton softball bats.

My trip was informative, and I was satisfied that they were a very high-tech and customer-responsive vendor. They further proved to me that they could manufacture in the quantities I required and I could afford to begin with. We figured out the lengths and sizes and kinds of inserts that we needed, and I was off to begin the Xtra Lite Displays® adventure for the next fourteen years.

## God Shows Up in My Business

As I began ordering poles and stocking them in my garage where the temperature varied depending on the time of the year in bone-chilling Minnesota temperatures that range from ten below zero to over a hundred, and it can change in a day or an afternoon over sixty-to eighty-degree differences.

I began attending as many small trade shows locally in Minneapolis as I could afford to expose my product to businesses and to test the market. One show I decided to go to a local balloon store and find the largest balloon I could get. I bought 3 of them and a small Helium tank. I blew them up and floated my display around the tradeshow floor holding on to a small ribbon while demonstrating that my display was the "Lightest Portable Display on the Planet". I know that I made a very big impression at that show. I usually picked up a few orders at these small shows; and being the only employee at the time, I was not only responsible to design them, market them, and manufacture them, sometimes all in the same day. I remember very well that I it was a very happy time in my life, as I finally felt after building each project a great sense of accomplishment and monetary improvement.

I had not yet caught on how to quite manage my inventory just right yet. With all the sizes and various parts I began to accumulate, it was becoming a very large task. I would initiate a sale, go off to my garage to build the display order, and all of a sudden, it occurred to me that no matter how many displays I built, I always had enough aluminum poles and accessories. One day as I thought about it for an instant, I realized that God had shown up in my business—and He became my business partner. Possibly just like he fed the five thousand with just a little boy's two small fishes and three loaves of bread. I was shocked at first and couldn't believe it, but whether it was absolutely true or not, I gave God the glory anyway and I began to see God as my business partner as he provided for me and my family in miraculous ways in those early days.

## Sales, the Spark of the Company Engine

One of my first customers was for a Christian company that worked in Bible translation. John, a former young missionary and indirectly a relative who just came back with his wife and family from Africa, was in need of employment. So I shared with him my new display product and offered him a sales opportunity, not a job as I wasn't quite ready for that just yet. As a great missionary who was used to talking and sharing with people, he set out to find companies who needed extremely light weight portable displays. He knew many Christian mission groups and just sat down and called them all. One of his first contacts he made was with a well-known Bible translation company who expressed their need for three hundred displays and graphics for their translators who would use them to build their support from churches and meeting for their mission work.

***Wow, what a boom!*** John got the order, and after we had it on the line, it was like catching an enormous ocean fish for the first time

*My Passion for Xtra Lite Displays®*

and not knowing how to safely get it into the boat. I thought about all the things I had to order and where I was going to get these banners printed. It was quite overwhelming as a first huge order. In a few days, I received their artwork and proceeded to find a good large-scale digital printer as they were quite new at the time in the late nineties. We had a sample printed and made the correct-sized display and sent it to them for their approval. They called back and said they absolutely loved it. I gave them the final invoice and then asked if they could send me 50 percent of the order up front. The next day, I received a wire for $85,000 the entire amount to my bank account. I sat down and took a couple of deep breaths. It was not only an order, but also a huge order with the funds to carry it through. It finally struck me that I was really in business for the first time, and boy, did it feel good!

## South Korea or Bust

I was told by REI that I should begin my investigation of suppliers by going to the Salt Lake outdoor and camping show in downtown Salt Lake City. It was a great annual event that we attended each year after beginning to order our tubing from Easton for several years.

However, after a few years and not being able to get our timing and payment plans in an acceptable balance, we realized that we were a small fish in a large pond owned by Easton. So we became extremely uncomfortable with Easton's slow and unacceptable ordering procedures and shipping dates of their products. We just could not see continuing to work with them. So we had to find another supplier. Easton's claimed that *"their product was made more superior than the aluminum from Korea, and it was brittle and not acceptable"*. However, as we looked into it further and met some of the South Korean companies at the Salt Lake camping show, we realized that they needed further investigation as to their quality and delivery capabilities as they appeared to offer many of the other benefits we were looking for such as fast delivery and product offerings and they seemed to be much closer to meeting our needs.

I called REI at their headquarters in Seattle and inquired as to who they were using in Korea, and they then told me there were several and that I should check them all out as they each had different products and techniques of manufacturing to offer. I then made a call and was able to connect with one of the largest of the aluminum tent pole plant managers and requested that I would like to come over and see his operations. I also mentioned that I knew there were at least two other plants and asked him if he could make the arrangements for me to visit each of his competition as well; and interestingly enough, he replied, sure, he would set it all up for me to make that possible.

I got all of my arrangements in order and actually took advantage of first stopping in Tokyo to visit with David Wright, our distributor there who was doing very well with connecting our products with a major photo printing company in Tokyo. They were Kodak's number one photo printer worldwide. I will discuss this part of the trip in another chapter.

## More Seoul in the Game

I took off on my first trip to investigate the three plants in South Korea. One of my additional incentives was that my son, then a second lieutenant in the US Army, *(now a Lieutenant Colonel)* had just arrived there a few months earlier on his first foreign assignment serving in South Korea. The hopes of being able to see him were high on my agenda as well. We were able to rendezvous at the Holiday Inn in Seoul, and he stayed overnight. The salesman from one of the companies offered to take us both to the *"Korean village,"* which demonstrated how the South Koreans lived with fully restored village scenes, portraying the early living conditions and culture of the original Korean people. We spent the day there, and that night, the driver volunteered to drive us up to Camp Casey where I stayed at my son's apartment overnight. The next day, I took the troop bus back down to Seoul with many soldiers on leave. My first stop in my company review included one of the largest suppliers of tent poles;

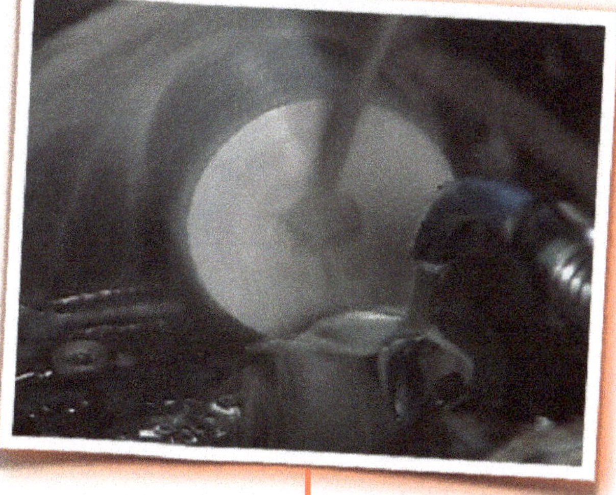

Cutting off a 6" dia. slice of Aerospace Aluminum ingot of high grade Japanese Aluminum that will be forged into a 1"x 10' long very thin and *"noodle like"* tube to begin the pultruding and shaping process.
Yunan Aluminum, Seoul Korea

**14**



however, they demanded a much larger order in the thousands, and even though their facility was very nice and new and in good order, they were making and expecting orders of hundreds of thousands. We were still in the start-up stage so it just wasn't a good fit for either of us.

The next company I toured was Yunan Aluminum. I was kind of taken aback by the first look at the facilities. It didn't help that it was a dark and gloomy-looking day. In many ways, it reminded me of back on my grandfather's farm with the strong smells and the sound of the machinery clanging in a rhythmic pattern. The extremely old dilapidated metal building, with everyone working there, was covered from head to foot in black aluminum dust and it looked like something out of the Korea war. I asked if they could point me to the men's room, and I found my first experience using a hole in the floor in an extremely dingy kind of bathroom that was kind of connected to the building that resembled more of an outhouse.

Les LaMotte with Mr Lee (R) on my first trip to South Korea to visit Yunan's original plant which he just purchased out of bankruptcy.

The businesspeople were all in a couple of mobile-home type building out front of the manufacturing building—normal East Asian fit and finish, which means not like anything at home. I was kind of beginning to wonder if I my long trip was a mistake. How could I trust my products, my business, and my family's future as well as my ever-growing number of employees to this half-baked old dirty technology place? I literally couldn't even believe it could be operational.

As we met with the owner, a very humble man, he appeared to be highly educated and confident, who could speak a little English, and his sales manager, who could speak a bit more. So somehow I managed to explain my needs to them both slowly and went through each detail to see if we were a match. When the president of the company showed me some of the samples of the final clean beautiful products, I started to relax. I found out they were making more than tent poles and in addition specialized aluminum products such as ski poles, walking sticks, and other beautiful and lightweight aluminum pole products for the huge Japanese walking and skiing market.

All I could say after visiting with them is that they in their own way were rather impressive to be able to produce such a highly designed and well-made product in such horrible conditions. I visited one more company. This one had its own distinct qualities. While I met with them, I could see they were hungry for my business, and they tried very hard to convince me that they were the ones to work with. I spent a little time talking to them, and then it occurred to me that they really didn't have even the facility of the last company.

Before I left Yunan, the owner noticed that I was a little uncomfortable about the present facility and quickly told me that they were in the process of building a new building and that the next time I came, it would be an entirely new facility.

So I gave him and his company the benefit of the doubt, and we began doing

Yunan's New very modern Corporate office out side the city of Seoul, South Korea.

*See the video of the plant: LesLaMotte.com.*

formal business together when I returned home. On our first orders, they did everything that I had requested and I couldn't have been happier with my choice. Once we got all of our signals together and could understand each other, they were excellent at keeping their pricing and delivery times in a comfortable and steady flow.

After a year or so, I went back to visit again and found them in an entirely new location and the company had modern facilities with a presence I thought I would never see. From the outside, I could see that a total transformation had taken place. Even the employees had corporate shirts on with the company logo. They took me to lunch at the corporate dining room, which to our standards wasn't bad, and all the working employees had company shirts and were even making their kimchi outside the lunchroom building, drying it on what appeared to be clotheslines. They all had stainless steel bowls of soup and chairs and tables to eat on, and I was so impressed with the transition I could hardly believe it. The manufacturing was even more impressive with automated sorters and straighteners going at full clip. However, the employees didn't look Korean; I found out they were from Vietnam as the South Koreans had already transformed their economy and most of the Nike shoe plants, which could be seen as these large empty warehouse facilities, were still there, but the manufacturing had already moved to China years ago.

Yunan workers feed 1" aluminum tubing to be *"pultruded"* down to 13mm, pickled, straightened, and anodized to give its beautiful and statin finish.

*See the video of the plant: LesLaMotte.com.*

Our relationship continued for many years, and it kept growing. Just before 9/11, we found out that we had not paid one of our major suppliers for a year and now we were behind and needed to pay $250,000 immediately. Since at that time that would have been about one-quarter of our total year's income and the total amount we spent on aluminum tubing in one year, what appeared like a boom had suddenly gone kaboom—and the effects of 9/11 took one more shot at our bow. We had just expanded our offices and invested in redesigning them and expanding our ability, and now both of these put us in a most difficult position. We were faced with having to look at letting go of almost all of our employees as our income stream was hit badly from the 9/11 incident. So instead of being able to enjoy my new office, I was forced to lay off my employees and go take up making and managing the entire business with my son Jordan, who was acting president at the time, and our graphic designer Rob.

## Recovery as the Buildings Fall

Jordan LaMotte, president of the company, and I found ourselves back to the same work as we started in our basement—cutting tubing, taking orders, making products, shipping them out the door. We did this for about another two years while we slowly paid off our huge debt to Yunan Aluminum and tried to meet the new space lease that doubled on our newly remodeled offices. Meanwhile, the orders for the product began to plummet as companies didn't know quite what to do in these new financial times where war was imminent. So most businesses tucked their heads in the sand and closed their purses and put a full stop on making promotional plans and slash their trade show budgets and weren't making new ones. This stuck terror in our nation's history but especially for us in a very unfamiliar and uncomfortable place of owning a business that just a few months earlier felt unstoppable and moving forward and now facing the ultimate disaster.

Robert M. Price - Former CEO of CDS, International Multifoods, Professor of Engineering at Duke University and Author of
*"The Eye For Innovation".*

14



***Chuck Casle***, Product Innovator for Control Data developed one of their first practical technology applications which propel the company forward while ***Seymour Cray*** *"The Father of Supercomputing",* worked for an additional 5 years on the first Super Computer. Later he split off from CDC and became the well known Cray Computers.

***Xtra Lite Displays*** developed this very unique display for CDC's 50th year celebration along with a history book and video held in Bloomington, Minnesota.

As owner and CEO of the company, we gathered our personnel left and inquired of our dealers across the world. Then we sat down and tried to make sense out of all that had happened. I needed a report of what they were hearing from some of our distributors, clients, and companies and if they were still making plans to attend trade shows or just reducing their budgets and packing it all in until it was all clear.

So the purchase of our original Xtra Lite Displays®, which at that time was selling with graphics for a full eight-foot exhibit for about $2,500 to $3,500 and before 9/11 were moving off the shelf at a high rate of speed because we had one of the most cost effective, compact, and lightest-weight displays in the world, which positively reduced both our clients' overhead and shipping costs. Soon companies really began to experience our displays as an extremely favorable option for their trade show usage and seeing us as a definite price and product alternative with Xtremely better design.

We even began selling to Skyline Displays® independent sales offices across the country and around the world. My former employer now had changed their owned sales offices to independent sales offices. Their display sales offices began to buy in larger numbers from us as Skyline Displays® had moved on to high-priced larger display systems and had nothing like our low-priced alternative.

However, with the 9/11 terrorist trauma and financial upset, it really put a scare into our customers. We were faced with digging in deep and going back to our beginnings to keep our company alive and afloat, at least keeping our doors open so we could hope for a quick recovery. After about six months, we knew it was not going to be a quick recovery at all.

## Starting Over with New Products

I brought out my design hat and went back to the "Skunk Works" and began to look at how to greater utilize our present technologies, parts, customers, distributors, and design a new product to market as a less-expensive display. What could we manufacture that was absolutely simple and we could make it for far less than $10 and sell it for at least three to four times the cost. We had just added an additional $32,000 digital printing plotter and laminator so we could be complete in-house digital printer and finisher. With the right new product we could increase our display and graphics sales netting us a definite price advantage and greatly increase our sales in these coming hard times.

I began by taking out a small project I was working on earlier and began to make some quick new prototypes to prove a new lower-priced metal based technology. We realized that if we could make a more cost-effective new display design made of only a few pieces of stamped steel, possibly we could remain in business and eventually gain some traction back as things began to change. We had to prove to ourselves that it was everything we thought it could be and deliver a solid dependable alternative just like our present world class display after all we did not want to ruin our good names we had established since our beginnings in 1997.

We found a local metal fabrication house in Lakeville, Minnesota, who would make a few finished quality samples to test and send to some key distributors for their review. If we could prove its overall effectiveness, then we could re-jumpstart our market and possibly begin looking for a partner in China that could make them at an even better price and in higher quantities, but with the same quality.
We also became very aware at the trade shows that everyone was going to China at the time to get *"more bang for their buck"* and unfortunately China was delivering quite well.

## Sourcing Sheet Metal in China

We began to try to find a metal fabricator of quality metal products in China that could make this new display at a an even less-expensive price and at greater volumes. We found a possible Chinese sheet metal supplier by asking our other contacts in China. We made contact and sent our designs over via email and in a few weeks received their first prototype back. However, after all the waiting, our hopefulness was

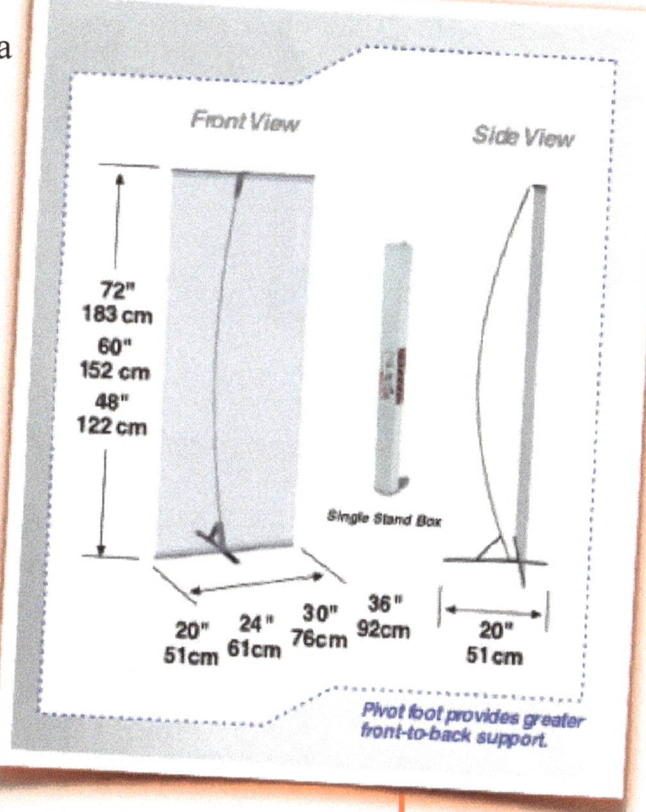

immediately dashed as they simply could not make a product out of the thickness of metal we had specified. It was, as normal, too flimsy and not stable enough as our American-made prototype. We needed a heavier-gauged steel; plus they said they could do powder coating, but they sent it to us just spray painted. We absolutely needed the powder coating. I knew it had to be powder coated as I learned from working at Skyline Displays that the powder coating added a thick plastic to the paint making the product feel and respond better with a velvet touch, and increased the overall fit and finish removing all the sharp edges. The Chinese failed the initial test miserably, but we had to continue to solve this product delivery system to market so we moved back to focusing on our American supplier.

## American Made – the Only Answer

We quickly went back to our local metal shop in Lakeville and asked them to consider making limited runs of the product making enough to bring the price more inline and we signed a buyout agreement to order products on demand and they would hold the balance on their shelves. This allowed us to buy them on an on-time basis. When they reached the need to remake, they were to give us a call and we could place an additional order guaranteeing them that they could begin building them again. We also went back to the drawing board and asked them what we could change on the design to make it simpler to manufacture and yet satisfy our needs of strength and guarantee our customers it would work perfectly every time. It proved to do all of that was required and more. Soon it began to fly off the shelves extremely fast as we had hit the right product with the right price for our distributors and their clients in just the right time. We learned that by becoming more aggressive and making bold changes in light of difficult circumstances can payoff greatly! We also looked at our retail sales pricing structure and soon we could begin to predict how many over how much time we would need to reorder. Since they were only a few miles away, we could reduce all shipping charges and pick them up ourselves as needed. This allowed us to meet a very slim but acceptable overall product margin, including the sales of custom graphics with it.

This one new product allowed us to update our brand and increase product offering and cash flow so we could continue to be competitive in the display marketplace. We continued to ride on all of the great marketing and branding we had built for the prior four to six years. In addition, it continued to capture more market share worldwide. It turns out this was the product the market determined was the right product for the right price, and we had to continually make reorders of them. In the end, we had made all the critical calculations for our customers and served them Xtra Lite Display® Innovation and success with a new less expensive product.

Soon, we began selling them in the thousands, increasing our printing, which increased our revenue and reduced our work load as we did not have to add any labor to this new product. The end result was increasing worldwide traffic once again.

Moving fast and nimble in producing a new product kept us on the road going forward even if slowly in some very debilitating and long dry times. In the end, it kept us out of closing our doors and brought us back from the dead, you might say, and saved our distributors' base from moving on as well to Chinese products.

We also employed a significant conversion ratio to reduce our retail pricing structure with a formula that allowed us to reduce our overall pricing very slightly to ensure enough profit but lower the wholesale and retail price. This worked very well and put us back on an upward direction and sped up our product sales.



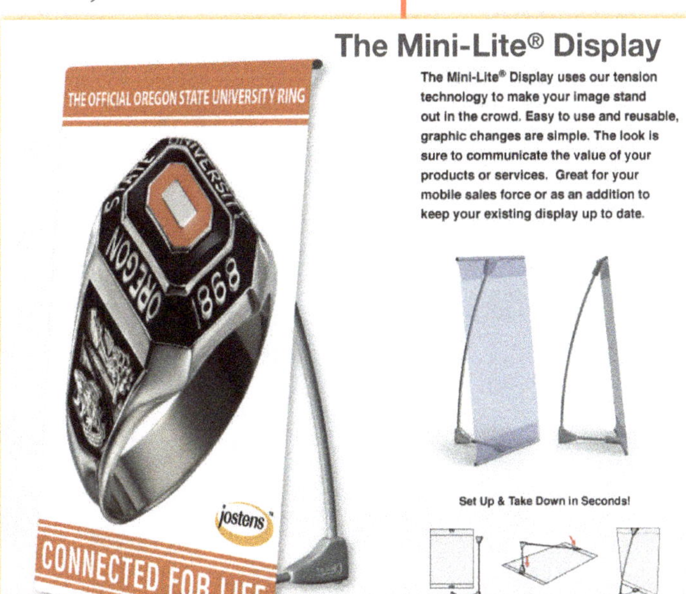

**14**



## Interruptive Distraction Appears

Unfortunately, just when you think everything is going well, watch out because there are other people ready to steal your lunch. My former employees we had to let go because of the sever income cut off, after they had collected their months of government checks, decided to start a group and work together. While working at Xtra Lite, they observed that we were producing about one-third of our income from our graphic print production. They had tasted our winning impact at Xtra Lite Displays® and wanted to find their own fortunes and formed their own graphics and display distribution business. They had heard of all of my life lessons and thought they knew all of my insider tactics and business plans.

They began in a small office space a few miles away and went out and started trying to sell graphics using competitors *"cheap"* display stands that we're entering the market with the tons of insanely priced Chinese products which were entering into the global display markets everywhere.

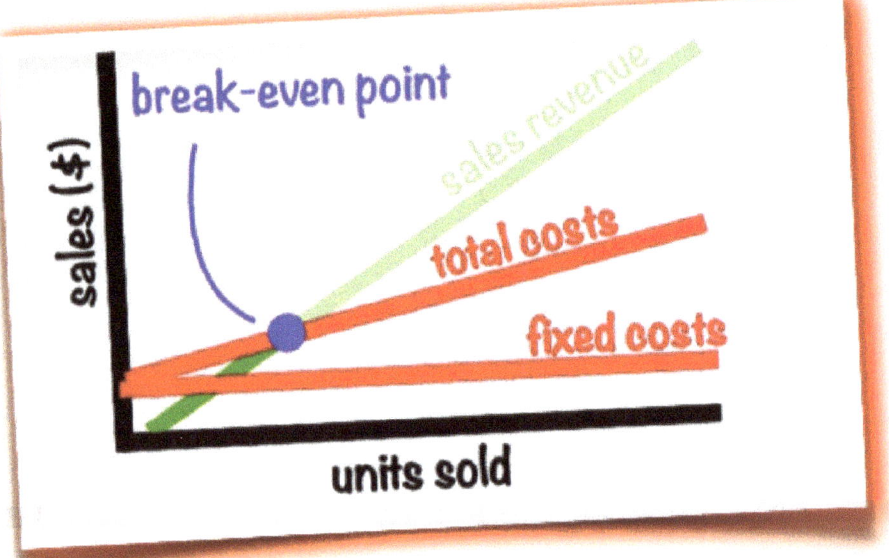


Understanding and using and establishing the principles of *"Break Even Point"* are absolutely essential if you plan on staying in business.

*Study.com/academy/lesson/how-to-calculate-the-break-even-point-deinition-formula.html*

They pooled whatever money they could muster and invested in their own digital printer and the computers to fire it up. As with all companies, they started up and began to see some income; however, they were not prepared for keeping it running, and their income to spending ratio got out of balance very quickly and it was soon headed for disaster.

We began suspecting that our designer, Rob, was moonlighting and also was doing the graphics for the other company and was a shareholder. We could kind of see the deteriorating work and attitude of Rob, and we knew we had to put an end to it. To keep our relationship solid with him because we genuinely cared for him and his new family, I found out about their company falling on hard times and so I took him out to lunch. While we were ordering and getting ready for a nice lunch, I asked him point-blank what was really going on with their graphics company. He finally reluctantly told me that they had basically given up and we're going out of business already. He told me that the spin-off graphics company was a "very poorly planned endeavor, at best." A couple of factors that really killed it quickly were first the lack of commitment from some of the partners, leading to a nonexistent and uninterested sales force. Secondly, the timing of the start-up relative to world events of 9/11 that severely changed the market itself for years, if not permanently.

However, because there were still bills to pay, he was working nights to try to keep the printer going and some kind of income stream still flowing. I looked at him and said, *"What can we do to get you all out of this mess because we value your work here with us too much? It is very obvious that you are not making us happy and apparently you are not making yourself happy, and you are working yourself to death."*
I proposed to him to try to convince the others to allow Xtra Lite Displays® to buy their debt out at this point and save them from further financial ruin. I asked him to prepare a spreadsheet of all their debt and assets and present it to me for our consideration. Jordan and I sat down and realized that basically they really

*"In any case, dissolving the company via the Xtra Lite Display's buyout offer was definitely the best thing that could have happened for me."*

*(–Rob Bartlett, Xtra Lite Displays graphic designer for over 12 years")*

weren't worth that much on paper, but with the prospect of us losing our designer, Rob, we realized we could benefit from adding their digital printer and small laminator. We quickly counted up the cost, and it came to around $35,000.

A month prior, we spoke to a fellow that came by our office occasionally as a client who offered to give us a lease on any assets we needed to continue our business. Interestingly enough, the money donor was my former boss at Skyline Displays®, who, after leaving, had acquired a nice payoff of funds and was loaning them out as leases to local businesses.

We inquired if they would agree to this purchase-of-assets sale, and we did the deal in a matter of only a few days. It solved two problems that were developing, and in doing so, we were able to solve both potential oncoming train wrecks. So we received the lease funds and purchased our former employees' business and wished them well. We genuinely hoped it would help them to see that being in business is not as easy as it appears to be and that with the good times come some bad times, and you must be ready for both. The ones that learn early continue for another day in business.

The additional printer began to give us shorter turnaround times and increased our graphics revenue stream, which was already a known quantity and structure within our business. The purchase was a good one for all involved.

## Restoration After a Long Recovery

After about six months, we began to see a slow but then a total recovery, and we celebrated the day we could write the big check to our South Korean supplier and get things straightened out and begin turning over a new leaf.

Very shortly after that, we saw our business begin not only at the original level, but also increase at an acceptable income to expense ratio, better delivery times, and a new larger showroom space.

While prior trials were all coming to a close, we were able to take one of the employees back working with us part-time again, and we to patched up some of the messy loose ends with some attitude adjustments and acceptance and recognition. I know that at least they respected what we had done to get them out of a bad situation. Over time, they became more loyal and hardworking and fully restored as a part of the team spirit once again.

## Streamlining the Production Flow

I was convinced that instead of paying for this large space that was now cut up and very inefficient, which limited our ability to move product and people through the right process of manufacturing. I began looking around for a possible alternative. The idea of office /condo space was kind of a new idea and one came available on County Road 42, which was becoming a major east-to-west highway. The idea was to take one of our largest expenses and shift it to one of our largest assets with potential recovery of at least some of our money in a future sale of property or company if we needed to grow our space any further in the future.

## Let's Use Our Pencil

Our present lease was at that time $6,500 per month or $78,000 per year, a long way from our first portion of the space of $2,500. The cost of our new office condo's mortgage would be $78,000 per year plus a down payment of $85,000. Sounds like a no-brainer, right? Lease and throw your money away every month and year, or try to recoup it by owning the office /warehouse condo building and renting from yourself?

We also needed $85,000 of cash down in order to make the purchase, which included the build-out costs. I found out that my house equity had risen substantially, and we had $85,000 available, so I took a second mortgage on our house and received the $85,000 to make the down payment on the condo building.

We arranged for Xtra Lite Displays to pay me via my new corporation and it would then pay down my second mortgage per month. The mortgages that we wrapped together on my house began to build equity with the money that we borrowed. I then set up a separate second corporation that then held the building outside of the corporation allowing more freedom to deal with the building as a separate corporation.

**14**

*My Passion for Xtra Lite Displays®*

The second corporation made it easier if we wanted to sell the building separately from Xtra Lite Displays® in the future. We then applied the $85,000 as my personal money shown as equity in my second corporation, which held ownership of my office/warehouse condo. Xtra Lite then paid my second corporation the lease amount per month, and the second corporation paid the mortgage automatically each month out of its own bank account. *(View the space design on page 162).*

## In Search of a New Office/Condo Space

I was able to find just such an expansive space very close to our present offices, and one which was just being carved up out of an older large prestressed concrete structure with twenty-two-foot clear ceilings. I immediately fell in love with it despite the numerous boats and trailers and the fact that there weren't any windows yet. I could envision it giving us the chance to experience every day the normal height and space of an actual trade show space. In many of our prior searches for space, almost all the spaces were cut up into small sales rooms with finished drop ceiling, and to remove them was cost prohibitive. This warehouse open space would offer us visual space and give our products the realism for our customers to experience their selection of our products in an actual trade show environment. It also would afford us the ability to begin looking at taller and higher solutions and begin to demonstrate overhead hanging and spinning display that the trade show market was beginning to call for. We could display our prototypes and could experiment with them and perfect their look and perk our customers' interest in them when they came in and for shooting our hero photos for our catalogues.

> *"After seeing this space, I figured it had everything we were looking for and it was a positive sign to move forward to investigate the building on County Road 42".*
>
> *(– Les LaMotte • Imagineer)*

I called the attorney who owned the building and asked if we could meet with him at the warehouse that noon. After looking it all over, kind of dirty, with boats and cars in storage in it with no windows, I saw the potential of windows and then realized that I needed the most eastern corner warehouse space. When he arrived and as we were discussing it, I asked if we could put about six or seven windows in it. He said they had already planned on putting in two levels of windows all the way around the building so that was a good response.

So he asked me, *"Well, do we have ourselves a deal?"* I held out my hand, never so sure of anything in my life and said, *"Yes, sir!"* He then told me that his people would get back to me with the paperwork. I countered by assuring him I would be designing the space and presenting the blueprints on the remodel to assure we could get everything we needed to make it all work. It was refreshing to be able to do a deal with a handshake. One lesson to be learned here is that the larger the deal, the less formal it usually is and the more the other party trusts you rather than a pile of paper and some signatures. I called Jordan and said, *"Son, come over and meet me here. I want to show you our new home for Xtra Lite."* He came over, and we looked around. He didn't quite get all the vision just yet, so we went to our local restaurant and I explained how we could make it work. We celebrated with a couple of small bottles of champagne and a toast. We kept the bottles in our offices to remind us that we had finally made it back into a strong enough position to be able to finally move forward once again.

I designed the interior of this 5,460 square feet of open industrial space. I hired my friend and architect Gary Turpening to come over and do the drawings of the building space, and I then scanned it into my computer and designed the interior walls and spatial use. Everyone in the company got excited and agreed on the design, and we purchased the condo. They began building and finishing the interior right away, and in approximately two months, we moved in. The floors in the front three-quarters of the building where epoxied so the entire floor was extremely smooth and easy to clean with just a wet mop like a photography studio. We laid carpet tiles in our twenty-by-forty-feet showroom space with black theatrical curtain hanging and movable on rails for the forty feet length. I had seen this while visiting a local warehouse it is a very reasonably priced way to finish a large warehouse space dividing the room visually and acoustics controlling our warehouse setting it visually a part from our showroom.

I was out shopping and met my old friend from Skyline Displays® who had just retired, so I scooped him up to help us.

His first task was to set up our warehouse as he did for Skyline for many years. He advised us that he had a friend that had all the upright steel shelving that would gave us forty or more racks for our inventory storage for free that was worth bring him on right there. I believe that just getting the newly built space that was set up for our workflow really helped us step up the workflow through it smoothly, and it absolutely looked impressive to our clients that we picked up an additional 20–30 percent increase in our revenue stream with many new customers who came in to see our showroom of products.

**Microsoft won an internal award for Best Practices**

Our best seller was our full 8' tall 10' trade show exhibit and its ease interchangeable panel design. The continuous header and matching graphic table allowed the user to have multiple exhibits with the same structural hardware and case.

We began to see a steady growth at our new office, and year after year, our sales despite our consistent and increasing customers, began to even out. So I personally began to go to more local shows and become more involved in our Burnsville business community and other business meetings in the greater Minneapolis area. The network that I was building began to pay off, and the global-reach strategy that we began to become more localized, but still with our dealers around the country and corporate and nonprofits scattered around the country. We now had better communicate both in visual and verbal with the entire team all in the same place and easy to get to. All of our offices in front were the new open-style environmental office with no ceiling, and our own custom-made conference table and media area, kitchenette, and all of our manufacturing took place behind the twenty-two-feet-tall black forty-feet theater curtain. I believe we began to have real curb appeal. It almost became automatic. Any company we could get to come down and see what we had to offer walked out with a sale. It was to their advantage as they could observe and test all of our standard products on twenty-by-forty-foot carpet tiled floor just like it would be at a tradeshow.

The Showroom space was right across from our offices and it speed up the adding of other kinds of structures and incidental products to fill out our full line of product offerings.

However, farther on the horizon out of the Pacific west came a tsunami that was building—the invasion of the Chinese into the global display industry. They hit the shores in mid-2005. It seemed almost too sudden; many different but similar Chinese solutions began to appear not only in our local market, but also at every show, such as the big ones in Las Vegas and around the world in Germany and even at the shows I attended in India.

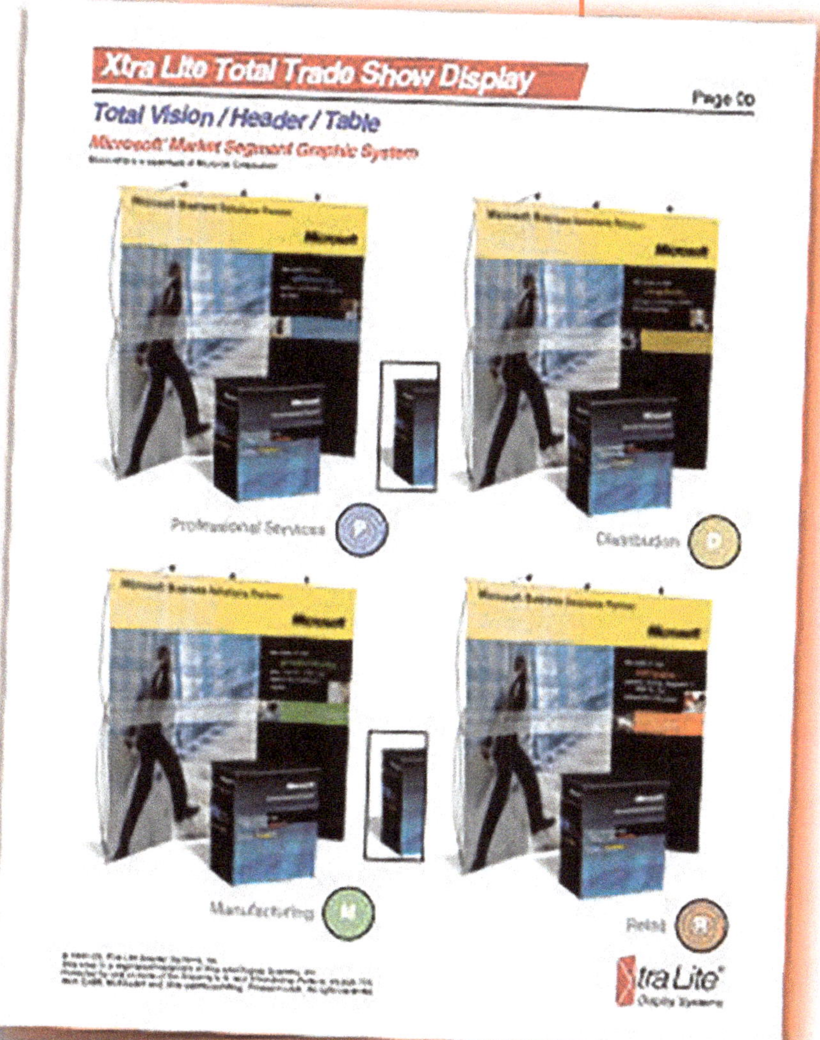


## The Chinese Invasion

It is my assumption that the Chinese had been going to trade shows all over the world for some time now and realized that what everyone needed was a low-cost trade show display solution. So they began making them by the thousands. The first product that appeared seemingly out of nowhere was the roll-ups, as they were called. They began to flood the trade show and event market everywhere. They quickly ate our lunch, even with our own US government despite the fact that we were one of the former best options for price and cost of shipping, however they being government and early in the *"we buy everything cheap from China"* mentality of the early 2000s.



*My Passion for Xtra Lite Displays®*

Xtra Lite's unique framework enlarged the marketing but shrunk the package size for Microsoft's flexible exhibit kit. They simply left the header, 2 of the 3 back panels and replaced one table graphic. Therefore by changing out just 2 panels they could pin point custom focus the exhibit products and services.

The Chinese knew how to put you out of business very fast—price, price, price, and it gets lower and lower. Why is that? Well, it took me taking a trip there to see it for myself. I found out why the Chinese can react so fast. The big dark secret is that the government will purchase the initial product design and tooling which is every businesses most costly investment of capital.

Then they make all of the parts available to hundreds of small cottage manufacturing shops around the country, much like Europe had in the '60s–'90s. These small companies would all make the same products or parts that became ubiquitous everywhere, and then these small shops could go and buy all the parts and begin assembling them with little to no overhead. Wholesalers would bundle them in to large sales forces, ready to take them globally around the world in every shape, size, and color to the trade show distributors, who because of the price and with no alternative but to purchase and resell them.

While I was in Shanghai, I visited with an attorney seeking to know how to keep my intellectual property safe working in China. They told me that Chinese product manufacturers only purchase a cheap *"design patent,"* which means if you make it just exactly like their design patent, they had some bite in their bark. I needed to know how their patents worked. They recognize design patents only, and they are relatively cheap compared to the over-eight years and $100,000 it took me to get my five patents. I could see that this was going to be very hard to maintain any rights to my patents there as many other companies worldwide have discovered.

## Why Patents for small entrepreneur's are generally not worth it unless they are a computer or healthcare device, service, or pharmaceutical company.

The minimum up front cost to suit is $250,000 per company per patent infringement. Now, consider that if the Chinese knocked off your product in their country, you fall prey to two factors. The first is that it is a normal practice for the Chinese to become exclusive manufacturers of US and other countries' products. The higher level manufacturers do a great job—if you call a 15 percent failure rate as good.

That rate has to be factored into anything that you buy from them. The second is that in every run they make of your product, they make a percentage for themselves without your knowledge to sell in China and other countries around the world.

So that is why they don't respect our patents and they can deliver and sell it so fast into every country in the world through their black market; you will never know what happened.
For example, when I was in Africa in 2009–2011 in South Sudan and Ethiopia, the Chinese had outlets selling look-alike iPhones and other cell phones. I know because I asked many people where they bought their iPhone there in Africa, and they responded at the cell phone store outlet.

I asked them if I could take a closer look at it as even from a distance it didn't appear to be anything like my iPhone. Sure enough, it was obviously a cheap knockoff because the fit and finish of the knobs and buttons on it and power-charging ports and cords were all different and not interchangeable with my actual iPhone.

Our most comprehensive catalog was printed in India. It required that I travel to India two times building a relationship. To get all of the files that were created into an Apple, I literally had to bring them one of our Apple computers so that they could make corrections and output the files to print it.

It ended up to be one of our best options as the printing was about one third of the cost to do in the US at the time.

In addition, we also built a relationship that included having one of our plastic parts that we could not afford the mold which was $5,000 in the US. We literally were able to get it made for less than $100 in India. I learned earlier product design work for Unilever that they made all of their molds in India for their complex bottles and sealing caps.

## Can't Beat'm Join'm

We really had no option but to join in. We were forced to embrace the Chinese-manufactured roll-up. They simply flooded the market in all the magazines and at all the shows, they were everywhere. The Chinese manufacturers were hungry to grow their business so we contacted a manufacturer and had them send some of their product to us for our inspection and testing. When we received them, we went about trying to see how we could improve on it and make it our own to fit our product line look and feel with special colors, finished plastic end caps with our name roll-up name on them. They sent us just raw extruded aluminum units with bolts and stuff kind of hanging out, kind of rough and crude to what we felt was our American customers' tastes and safety issues.

So we redesigned them and tried to breathe into them a new designer look and feel with improved performance of the back pole that it seemed all Chinese products were just drilled a hole in the aluminum and that was where the back pole was supposed to work. No wonder why they all suffered from our point of view, saggy and looking horribly unstable. After all, we had designed our Xtra Lite Displays to be the best dress display with tight graphics that stood strong and tall. The Chinese simply just slammed them on without regard to the overall fit and finish. We knew we had to overcome some of their built-in flaws, or we couldn't even think of promoting these cheap-looking cans of aluminum.

However, the one limitation was that the quality and thickness of the superior heavy-weighted graphics we were using was exactly opposite of their thin almost-see-through cheesecloth-type printed graphics. So we were forced to actually take apart every one we received to wind up the coil spring inside to give us more power to allow us to use our better-quality graphics.

So now our cheap Chinese roll-up became really expensive because we had standards for our selling to our customers. Every time you handle a product, you add cost to it. So as the progression goes, they kept sending us products that were broken in shipping because they had no idea of how to package them with enough cardboard, which usually requires two sets of boxes from China just because of the rough ride at sea and the abuse of handling them through our shipping services.

You also have to remember that their cardboard, which I discovered in South Korea, is not made like ours of virgin wood fibers. It is made from who-knows-how-many-times recycled cardboard fibers and, yep, you guessed it—human waste. Ever wonder why all Chinese shipping boxes look like they are going to fall apart when you look at them? It is because they will, and they do. You know where they come from by the strange yellowish color of their cardboard, not the nice rich brown wood strong fibered stuff we make here. The Asians have wimpy soft flutes on the inside and paper-thin yellow paper hardly enough fiber compared to ours know wonder they fall a part before arriving.

The other problem we had was we had trouble keeping the right widths of the displays in stock. So after some investigation, we figured out how to just buy two sizes and then cut them down to the customer's desired size. We know that our service this way was totally unique in the trade show world, so we continued to move more inventory because we were the only ones with the right graphic width available, which gave us another "sticky" point in our marketing.

Once we were able to begin seeing a consistent product manufacturing of the new product we had designed and detailed, we began selling discounted samples to our distributors and our US dealers before they started to find other half-baked Chinese products. We were concerned that if they began

14

My Passion for Xtra Lite Displays®

Les LaMotte designed this Skyline Displays® trade show exhibit ad used in all inflight magazines in the late 80's. Skyline invested $2-3 million per year in inflight magazine ad placement. Great Plains Software eventually grew rapidly and became Microsoft in Fargo ND and eventually one of our clients. I am sure this ad because of its frequency played a role in their success.

buying the cheap roll-up, it would reduce the overall quality distinction we tried so desperately to build into our product's branding for many years, therefore watering down our entire quality presentation platform to simply price.

We held on by the hair on our teeth for about a year or so, and then we began to see our sales plummeting even in the roll-up area as the Chinese continued to pull the strings tighter around our neck.

## Chinese Products Pour In

Even the US government instead of purchasing our American-made and promoted banner stand, they purchased the Chinese-made roll-ups after 9/11 as they built up the TSAs in airports. Nice free advertising paid for by the US government in the airports where every business in America saw the roll-ups every time they entered an airport. The exposure was very similar to a strategy I had used twenty years prior in consistently placing ads in airline magazines for Skyline Displays® to the tune of three million per year. These ads that I designed and placed put huge pressure on every businessperson en route to their trade shows across the country and exploded Skyline Displays® fast growth.

Now, the Chinese by default or by design were using the same high pressure advertising technique and getting paid to do it everywhere in the United States and around the world without paying a dime but instead got filthy rich in a flash.

The Chinese continued to drive a huge wedge into Xtra Lite Displays® around the world at a price point undercutting all other product pricing, even other US or European products around the world. The Chinese roll-ups and other products inundated every worldwide market overnight and were sold for one-tenth of our Xtra Lite Displays® price and most of all other display prices, therefore completely eating everyone's lunch around the world before we could do anything about it..

Did they do everything that our Xtra Lite could do? No, but the consumer quickly forgets the benefits of your product, seduced by the cheap prices offered by the Chinese invaders.

So I kept asking myself why on earth would the Chinese enter the world market and completely ignore a sales technique of just slightly selling under the other products pricing? Why would they just leave all that money on the table. I just shook my head.

If they would have really researched the market, they could have made tons of more money much quicker, but they wanted to totally toss everyone out of the ball game and own the entire market with their cheap pricing.

They obviously were not interested in our business approach, their approach of total price reduction had been used for over 4,000 years. They also were not concerned about quality, variety, usefulness, an investment concept like the United States and Europe's were used to in all business. Nor are they particularly concerned about being sued for product performance because what I discovered is that all of their products are made by cottage industry throughout the country and so no one company is totally responsible for the results and the cost of legal action impossible.

It was extremely unlike how Xtra Lite Displays® was pursuing, a seamless connection between graphics to give our customers the effect of a solid trade show exhibit that was extremely well priced and lightweight and working so well.

I am sure their reasoning was that since they already owned the tooling, it was extremely practical to just take movie screen mechanisms they had been manufacturing for many years and simply turn them upside down and add two swing-out feet bars for balance and a cheap folding aluminum or steel pole up the back to hold the graphic up rather badly as it relied on the person putting it up to make sure it was tight, and of course, most people could care less about adjusting it or really know how to do it. Did it look as professional as ours? No, but for a lower price, people will drastically change their principles and throw out the old concepts and move forward with new challenges if they actually perceived them as missing. Most of those who bought into the first roll-ups could have cared less; they just wanted a faster, they believed easier, and cheaper banner stand solution—period.

As they say, that's what the customer wanted, and that is exactly the low standards by which the Chinese conquered the entire banner stand new digital graphics world in only a few years. So now what were we going to do? Do we buck the Chinese wave or join it and ride it out? From our point of view, they were much larger, and we just kept going forward, offering our Xtra Lite Displays® as long as our customers were still purchasing them even though we could soon see our worldwide presence begin to dwindle in numbers and profitability.

## Finding Our Chinese Connection

We first made our connection with the Chinese company on the Internet as an email from an inquiry by a businessman from Singapore. His business was marketing shipping containers. He said that he was coming to the United States with a fellow businessman from Shanghai. So I told him about an exhibit in Chicago at the same time, and he agreed to come by our exhibit there to see our products.

This Chinese fellow in a brown corduroy suit came by and just about knocked me down while he was trying desperately to say hello but is so excited that he can't help himself. I realized it was our new friend from China so I welcomed him into our exhibit to see some of our Xtra Lite Display products. His interpreter friend said that they would be coming to Minneapolis in a few days and wanted to meet with us at our offices.

So I scrambled to find a translator to hire because he didn't speak any English and I obviously didn't speak any Chinese. I explained to him that he would have to pay for the translator because we didn't know what kind of relationship we had just yet. So he agreed and we had a lunch and dinner to get to know each other better.

It turns out that the translator ended up to be a good connection because his company was sponsoring several speakers from China who were businessmen, government officials, and diplomats. I was invited to many speaker sessions and some dinners to meet with the government officials firsthand. I received a lot of business data and just how their thoughts about and conducted business in China.

We were in the office trying to communicate after the translator left. I said that we were looking to make a new case and used my body language to show him our present case we had made in Italy. He wanted to have one to take with him, and I agreed he could take one. I tried to ask him to give us a quote on the making of the mold for our possible new work as he wanted to market our product in China.

He took the case with him to China, and within a few weeks, he wrote me an email saying that they had the mold ready and then I realized that, he didn't understand what I was trying to tell him about getting a quote rather he thought I wanted him to make it for me. Well, to my complete surprise, he did. The only thing that I had asked him for was the price. Now that he had the mold done, he was expecting an order.

Meeting with my Chinese partner company in
Shanghai. Interpreter on my Left and to the Left
of her is the President of the company.

The shocker came when I received an email from the Italians, which was quite authoritative and they accused me of going to China and making the same product. I was totally taken aback. First, the mold maker in China was totally unaware that Xtra Lite Displays® already had an agreement with the Italians for the United States and everywhere else except Europe, and he never inquired for any rights to make it in China. He assumed the rights to move forward without my consent. Then the plot thickens.

Our new partner in China wanted to sell some so without telling me, he brought some to a show in Germany, possibly Düsseldorf Messe, and the Italians saw the product there with a Chinese

company selling it. They then sent me a letter and said that our agreement was all messed up and they weren't going to sell to me anymore and accused me of going to China to get it done behind their backs.

My agreement with the Italians who were making it was that I would buy a set amount of them each year in order to pay down the mold costs. I had already invested about $20,000 in making the mold with the Italians. We had agreed to having the rights to United States and everywhere else in the world that we sold our Xtra Lite Displays®, but we couldn't sell it in Europe.
We had no intention to sell it in Europe, and this less-than-savory first arrangement with China turned out to be a very sticky one at best and gave us a negative position with our Italian partner.

## Gathering Distributors

### The Key to Disney

Having designed and patented a product that solved one of my childhood hero's companies needs after over 50 years is just one more small assurance to me and wonder, a badge I have collected in my life that confirms that I have arrived having spent my life as an Imagineer.

So how did a company that famous, huge, and financially sound want or even know about a small boutique upstart entrepreneur guy like Les LaMotte in Minneapolis? Normally, you would think that you just pick up the phone and ask for an appointment to see the head of Disney's marketing department. Well, you could, but since I was there making a presentation to Universal Studios as well, I just found out where their offices were in Orlando and took my rental car and drove over to ask to see someone.

*Proactive business client contact procedure:*

- Go online and do some reach on the company you wish to contact.

- Call and ask for the person responsible, in our case, marketing.

- If the person you are trying to reach is not available, leave a voicemail.

- If you are in their offices, then leave your standard sales materials.

**15**



***What's Really Happening:***

- They don't know who you are or what your product can do for them.

- Hey, what's the matter with you anyway? Don't you know this is Disney? (That's what it felt like any way.)

- Possible that they have no interest in following up with you no matter how many times you try to contact them and each time you try, they build a larger wall against your insistence.

- Leaving your materials is absolutely worthless as they see their filing cabinet for these as a file thirteen or the closest waste basket.

My childhood dreams of working with my Disney idol seemed to be disappearing, and maybe I failed in my approach, or my product just wasn't good enough and my product really didn't have as many benefits and appeal as I thought it did. Many questions go through your mind in a moment like this. I learned to just keep walking and go to the next potential customer. Several months go by, and I suddenly hear from our Japanese distributor that a show was coming up in Tokyo and he described that he was going and making a big impression there with the Xtra Lite products. Turns out very positive, and it was well received by customers and even the government of Japan. After the show, he was so excited he called me and told me that not only was it a success at the show, but he could hardly talk as he said that Disney came by his booth and was so interested they made an instant order for hundreds of our XL1 banner stands and not only that, but that the entire East Coast marketing organization responsible for doing trade shows around the world made our display the only one that any company could use and they bought hundreds as well.

Les LaMotte in Tokyo with David Wright our Japanese Distributor and his Xtra Lite Display clients.

So you can imagine that both he and I were totally shocked and dumbfounded at this news, especially by Disney, as it was only a few months earlier that I had been to see them in Orlando. The extremely interesting part was that their interest came from the fact that they saw it at a Japanese trade show and that is why they liked it. I found out afterwards that the Japanese are the most picky at buying products from other countries and that they're liking my Xtra Lite Display® product, was a huge win in itself. At that time, the Japanese purchased less than 10 percent of their products from outside of Japan.

David met with the country of Japan's tourism, and they purchased hundreds of our XL1's to promote *"Hello Japan,"* a government PR effort to have a nicely dressed white gloved young woman greet everyone that got off the plane in their airports to promote the country of Japan.

## Next Stop, São Paulo, Brazil

My trip to São Paulo Brazil was a wonderful adventure. My new distributor there was found in a very funny yet historical way. My friend from college, now navy commander, was telling me about the size of his yacht he wanted to purchase and mentioned that it was made in Brazil that he was looking at purchasing because of the size and price. So I went online to see it and sent an inquiry email. I received a strange email back and it said, *"Are you the one who made Xtra Lite Displays®?"* I thought for a moment and then said, *"How do you know about my Xtra Lite Display® products?"* His answer is that he was one of my former distributors in Brazil and had started selling our display products way back in the beginning of early 2000 after we became a corporation. Then I finally made the connection—he ran a Mercedes-Benz showroom and used our banner stands exclusively. I told him we were looking for a new distributor in Brazil, and he volunteered to put me in touch with his good friend and their family was in the digital printing business and they were looking for a banner stand product to represent in Brazil. He said he would give me a good reference and so I called to inquire of their interest. Within a week, I received an email the father of the family printing group. He told me he had established several creative businesses, including design and digital printing. They were very interested in me coming down to visit and eagerly wanted me to bring samples of my Xtra Lite Display® products. He further expressed a keen interest in representing the product there in São Paulo.

São Paulo is an extremely large and beautiful city of over 17 million people and is one of the largest cities in the world with a real poverty-class challenge. The father had assigned the Xtra Lite Display's® business to his youngest son who also had a young family. Very industrious family as his young wife was a very accomplished pottery maker and painter. She gave me one

**15**



of their son's birthday additions that she would make for all of her friends and familia for his birthday as gifts. They surprised me on Sunday on a trip to an all-you-can-eat Brazilian barbecue *"churrasco"* for lunch, and wow, was that great! I quickly found out that a picanha is a cut of beef called sirloin cap rarely used in the United States as it is cut into other cuts such as loins for us. Everyone barbecuing and serving the meat there were dressed in the traditional Gaúcho Pantaloon pants. Gaúcho in Portuguese stands for skilled horseman, reputed to be brave and unruly, which sounds like the American cowboy to me. Which adds to the complete flavor, which is absolutely Brazilian and wonderful. There are Brazilian barbecues here in large cities scattered around the United States. You control how much you eat with little square chips of wood painted on one side with red and the other green. You put these colored chips down next to your plate every time the Gaucho *(meat carver)* comes by with the freshly barbecued meat on a sword, they would see the color of wood cards. If it was red, he wouldn't offer you any of his meat. If it was green, he would start to peel off thin cuts of the most juicy and the most wonderful aromatic seasoned beef you have ever eaten. Heaped on your plate right in front of you, how cool is that! Just a wonderful experience, and

if you have not tried it, you will have a hard time stopping. We had a few great days together checking out the potential business opportunities and one night he took me to his friend's two-story modern driving range like the ones I had seen in Japan. So I drove a few buckets of balls and had a great time as it was the owner's birthday and there was plenty of food. I couldn't help realizing that the owner was so handsome.

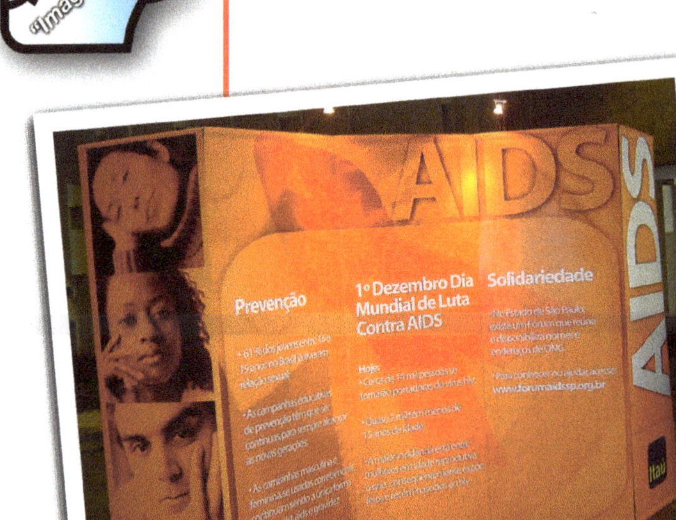


São Paulo, Brazil
AIDS for IntegRHa

I told him he needed to come to Hollywood as they would cast him right away in some kind of movie. He and all his guests laughed, and we had a great time together. The potential distributor had his eyes on something else and showed me the location in this new golf building. I could see his creative juices were on the boil, and he introduced me to a large wall where he saw filling it with many of our Xtra Lite wall mount displays. I agreed and quite enjoyed his insight and eye for sales.

The highlight of my trip there was when our new distributor friend invited me over to his family's house in Albertville, which is a very wealthy area north of São Paulo. I was amazed when we arrived; it was like I had stepped into one of the wealthy neighborhoods in Minneapolis like Edina. Nice homes, great roads, nice schools, extremely different from the downtown areas among the poor in São Paulo. I had a great time getting to know some of his relatives and seeing firsthand how a Brazilian family works together enjoying each other, and it kind of felt very much like home with the relatives. The language was certainly not the same even though they spoke exceptionally good English, but the warmth of the people was wonderful and, of course, the food was out of this world!

The next day, I touched base with a wealthy banker I met in Jamaica at an international business group meeting a year before. He was very gracious and invited us downtown to the Wall Street of Brazil. My new distributor friend was very impressed. He asked us to meet in the top dining area of the building close by his office. After treating us both to a great lunch, he took us down to the actual trading floor at the stock exchange, and we got to see the São Paulo version of the NY stock exchange where it all happens. That was very cool, and then he took us to his offices and we met people in his investment banking company.

While we were beginning to leave, he asked if I could come to his home in Albertville to have dinner with his family that evening. I mentioned that I didn't have a car, and he said not to worry, his driver would pick me up at the hotel. We arrived very late that evening but had some great conversation with another friend he invited over. I found out in our conversation that he was the president of one of the largest telecoms in the world and so I also spent some time getting to know him. Of course, his beautiful wife and several children were there, and we sat down to a wonderful meal and had some wine afterward. It was a one-in-a-lifetime experience. The next morning, my new distributor and I visited some of the companies that he had references to possibly buying Xtra Lite Displays®. They were extremely impressed that the designer of the product would come to their country to demonstrate the product.

Later, we explored another opportunity. This was a real eyeful. In order for us to enter this business office there in Brazil, we had to offer our hand for fingerprints, our passport, I had to have a picture taken, and walk through a metal detector. I felt like I was going through customs or my prior experiences going into prisons. That is what it took for us to just visit a design company there. I will never forget how extremely hard it was to do business with all the security present. I was gaining great respect for my future distributor's abilities to work through those kind of

Xtra Lite Displays® first Exhibit in Mumbai India in search of distributors. The entire exhibit fit into just two Xtra Lite large cases.

hoops and steep learning curves for me just to do some business.

As we left for the airport, I got an even greater surprise. This young man, soon to be our distributor whom I had just recently met, told me that he and his wife were going to search out a new church after they had been around me for a few days. My faith in Christ and reliance on God was so evident that they told me they had been drawn closer to the person of Jesus and realized that their lives weren't where they should be with God. I assured them that they had made the right decision and I was extremely happy that they felt that way about our visit. I was overjoyed that I now had a wonderful company and family group to represent my products and that my life had touched them so deeply. That day, I returned home and in ten hours after a quick repack and some shut-eye, in the morning, I took off for my first trip to Mumbai, India, another twenty- two-hour international flight to another city of over 17 million people.

## Finding New Markets in Our Backyard

I had met the retail marketing design coordinator of Best Buy, back when I left Skyline Displays® and was beginning to expose and market my Xtra Lite Displays® at local trade shows

to get the reactions of companies to the product and initiate some sales. This young designer became very interested in what I was doing and wanted to know more about my Xtra Lite Display® product as I got the impression he had been following my success with the company.

Some years later, he came by our booth at a large show we were exhibiting in Chicago. We had pulled out all the stops, and we invested almost $20,000 for this show, probably the most we had ever invested in a show as it was one of the largest for the retail marketplace. I recognized him walking by and spoke with him, quickly filling him in on our product's progress and how our company was continuing to develop. He was very impressed and asked me to call him when I got back home as he would like to explore a possible idea he was working on with me.

I went to see him at their retail fulfillment building in Edina, He was so extremely interested at how our product worked and asked if I would put together a specific solution to what he wanted that looked impressive, was extremely portable, and yet compact and lightweight and could be packed up and shipped to the next location. I asked him for more details as to what they would be using it for. He revealed that they needed temporary rooms for interviewing new candidates for hiring employees in Best Buy stores to replace their present HR displays made of PVC and cloth graphics. When they had hired all of their employees, there was no room to store them or need for the immediate future use so they just threw them away. I later found out that it was costing them $1 million a year to make and throw them away with a net loss of one million dollars per year.

Realizing this was a rather cool opportunity to demonstrate how our product could be used in an entirely new and possibly expansive secondary market, I put together a plan using our Xtra Lite Displays® with their unique ability to instantly connect a series of banners together and build any geometric shape by our patented universal *"snap-together connectors"*.

I proposed the idea to them in semi 3D drawing form and emailed it off to him for review. He loved the idea and called me immediately and asked me to come in as he had additional questions to ask me about my proposal. I answered his questions and he expressed high interest in the proposal. In fact, after getting more details and a preliminary pricing structure, he told me to meet him at their new main office on Hwy 494 the following week to sign the contract. This became one of our largest sales in our short history for over $100,000. I sent in our closer Jordan, over to do the paperwork and seal the contract. Their only stipulation was that we produce an instructional video on a DVD in both English and Spanish for each of the display case groups.

So Jordan agreed and sealed the deal. We made a full mock-up and demonstrated it to them with all the parts and cases, etc., in about a week. Jordan demoed it to the decision makers, and they all loved it and signed off on it.

With a smile, Jordan signed the contract and received a purchase order for our first of many $100,000 contracts from Best Buy. However, we found out we had to be on their outside suppliers' list, and that was a trick in itself to overcome. Because of the tightening of the grip on cash flow, they put a freeze on accepting new suppliers to limit the number of outside contractors. We, however, were given special permission to be added to their contracting supply list. Now, the only thing we had to accomplish was how to get at least half of the money to buy all the materials and pay our people to build them.

Our salesperson, Tom, had a very strong background in high finance and was a CPA. This was one of the reasons I had hired him, as his family was going through special medical circumstances with his beautiful wife who was extremely sick and needed a lot of his extra time and attention and for clinic visits. I offered him a flexible working arrangement as our salesperson with a floating schedule. This allowed him more time with his wife and his three growing children while she was receiving her medical treatments. Tom had worked with some very wealthy individuals, and he told us that he could approach one of them with our need for cash up front to swing the deal with Best Buy. He took the purchase order with him to his friend, and he agreed, unfortunately, to the tune of 10 percent interest. Which kind of took the wind out of our sails because we were hoping for something just a little more comfortable to help us out of our financial pinch. We agreed and received all the funds except the last 10 percent, which was held in suspension until we delivered the project in a few weeks. Best Buy then issued an invoice from Tom's contact, and Best Buy paid the funds directly to our third party. He kept the 10 percent that was withheld, and our debt was paid off. It all worked out very nicely, and we made some very big impressions with Best Buy. Over the next two years, they purchased another two purchases of the same, which allowed us the finances to repay our debt with our South Korean aluminum supplier and start over with a clean slate with them.

So it remains one of Best Buys, *"Best Buys"* and three times our *"Best Sales"*.

## We Weren't Left Behind

In 1998, we returned to the GMA, and this time we were packing my new Xtra Lite Display System. Just down the aisle from us from Indiana was the Cloud Ten film group who were eyeing our displays on exhibit. One of the owners, which I later learned was one of the producers, told me that he would like to look at using our display to release their new movie coming out in a few years called Left Behind, which became one of the first Christian-based films to hit the movie industry with actors I later learned were Kirk Cameron and Brad Johnson.

**Left Behind Film Promotional Video Tape Box Tower**
This unique tower structure was my second product that I developed from the original XL1 Display design. It was literally an *"X"* inside of a Square or Rectangular tube. This particular design was used at a trade show for new movie releases and we made it appear to be a giant Video Tape box which was the premier movie format available in the late 90's.

# 2008 Financial Meltdown
## Your Worst Nightmare Stares You in the Eyes

The death blow came in 2008 when the world financials hit an all-time low and the stock market fell off its hinges and the country and the world went into a complete meltdown after almost twelve years of sweating blood and tears to achieve a worldwide business, over 600 distributors around the United States, and 250 around the world. Our huge investments were now in real estate, equipment, inventory, relationships with hundreds of vendors and suppliers in three countries. We had business relationships we had fought for with major corporations, and they also felt the same jolt as the orders just basically quit coming in. We could only just stand there dumbfounded as our hopes to stay alive as a company were almost completely dashed. Only a few days after President Obama was elected, our monthly income plummeted to under one-third of our normal monthly income of around $85,000 per month to a $20,000 per month average. It simply left us breathless; it was as though someone reached out and punched us square in the face for a knockout punch. We then had to pick ourselves up off the floor and wipe away the tears and figure out where the bleeding was and try to begin to patch it up and figure out where major surgery had to take place to keep the patient alive and well in this new mangled business environment.

16



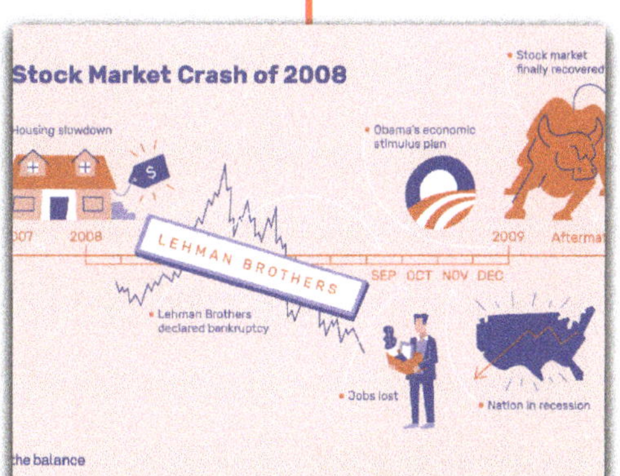

Here we were, with almost twelve years of business, and we had already endured two other huge punches of financial hits. Just how much more could we stand, and what were our options as the critical mass of our business began to wiggle and sway out of this massive and disturbing situation we found ourselves in? Of course, as we looked around, there were signs popping up all around *"for lease"* and companies just shutting their doors, and some never to be seen again.

There was an unholy feeling in the air, and people's attitudes began to change from extremely happy and pressing forward to extremely cautious and suspicious. Not knowing what else would befall them or their lively hood, there was definitely an air of gloom thick enough to cut with a knife all around you and in the business marketplace. Almost immediately, the world of advertising dried up, and the push for new marketing budgets vanished. The trade show industry all but stopped in its tracks. There was a certain repeat of what happened on 9/11, but it felt much closer to home as each person and business seemed to have been set afire and they were all burning at the same time. A certain senselessness to the whole thing prevailed with a stillness that could allow a pin to drop and be heard across the entire metro area and around the world.

It was nothing that I had ever experienced before in my life, not even 9/11. It was personal for everyone, and people were scrambling to figure out how to pay their mortgages and buy their groceries and pay their credit cards that they had leaned on way too hard in the prior year. A great sense of hopelessness prevailed.

## Help Came Out of the Blue

One day, Jordan received a call from our contact at Best Buy's offices, whom we had made all the displays for at Best Buy. They said they wanted to send a semi-truck to our warehouse full of our displays—in fact, all of them as we had sold them a few years earlier. The amazing part was that even though we had charged them about $300,000, they said we could have them all back *"free of charge"*. We knew they were hit hard like us during the 2008 disaster and this was their way of saying thank-you and helping us since we had helped them save almost $3 million dollars in the process over the last three years.

During the later parts of 2007 and in the summer of 2008, financial weakness began for many of our largest clients, and even Best Buy was just about brought to their knees. They had just undergone a two to three years' construction project of their new corporate new campus on the corner of 494 and 35W in Bloomington Minnesota. They also found that they had to begin laying off many employees. There was a general feeling in the air of instability in many companies it was becoming all too evident that something devastating was going to happen.

Jordan came in and told me what was going to happen, and we both were totally blown away—his response on the phone was, *"Sure, let us know when you are going to be here. We are ready for the delivery!"*

We rearranged our warehouse to accommodate all the product and cases that we could put back into inventory. The interesting thing about aluminum tubing is that because it is so resilient to any environment and that is why it is used ultimately on the best tents that mountaineers take on the highest mountains and work in harsh winds and rain, they don't deteriorate or even look dinged or used. We were not surprised that they were still in excellent shape, and we were able to recycle thousands of dollars of materials we could reclaim and turn them back into immediate profitability, which helped us stay alive during these extremely desperate days.

This huge return of product alone helped us by not having to buy additional new aluminum poles, and it saved us from reordering and the high cost of shipping from South Korea by FedEx and got us immediate access for new orders. We were able to recover almost 90 percent of all the parts and cases. Thank you, Best Buy, for your great gift, and it was one of the smartest things they could have done to minimize their waste by recycling it back to us in a meaningful way. Who says that large companies don't have a heart? We know that Best Buy certainly does! It was incredible, God had given us the opportunity to continue and satisfy customers with our Xtra Lite Display products once again without having to order new poles and undertake the high replacement costs at a time we could not afford to. This one act of reprieve allowed us to continue for the next two years— skinny, underpaid, but as a company. The immediate need to go through bankruptcy was temporarily avoided. However, temporary is temporary.

## I Made the Wrong Decision for Me

As I look back with 20-20 hindsight today, had I realized the full extent of our real condition and the eventual long recovery, I should have by all rights filed bankruptcy immediately in

December of 2008. The results would have been quite different for myself even if I was forced into retirement. In bankruptcy, we had most of our immediate debt in credit cards, which in bankruptcy is the best position, as they simply go away without protest. However, I would have been able to keep a large sum of money, the other 68 percent that wasn't taken in the stock market crash. So I learned a very huge lesson of not falling in love with your baby. Unfortunately, I had and was hoping especially that since it would affect my employees whom I had also grown to really love and respect, I just couldn't put especially my son's four children and them in a very difficult position at that time.

## The Inevitable Wolf at the Door

As we approached the end of January in 2011, we began to have to pay for supplies before we could get them, and our long fought-for good-credit position had sunk to a new low. The final death knell was the county demanding $29,000 of taxes for our building and business.

Being in business for only twelve years as a manufacturer, looking out the ship's window, I could not see land or know whether we were still upright or going down soon like the Titanic. Unfortunately, because I didn't have that many years in just business, I could not read the signs. After all, I had been trying to sell the company for a few years prior to this major hit. That was not going to happen in this new collapsing financial environment. There was nothing left to find as a solid mooring to safely tie us up in such a quick and hard-felt perfect storm. If I would have been more business savvy at the time, I would have immediately cut and run and took my losses at that point. I would have saved at least half of my IRA money, and I wasn't over sixty years old yet and maybe I could have taken a lesser job or gone back to just doing my graphic design again like I had for the first thirty-five years of my working life.

There were other factors fogging the windows of the ship—my son Jordan, who had assumed the helm at least a year or more before this, just had two more twin children. How could I as a father and grandfather possibly close the company down and cut my losses and leave him without a job in a moment when everyone else was losing theirs? Based on that dilemma and our track record, we soon recovered. I decided to continue and weather this what I thought at the time was a temporary storm like the two prior storms. I decided not to give up the ship just yet. We patched it up and sailed on for a few more years. Unfortunately, hindsight is 20-20, and from my present perspective and knowledge I gained, it was the *WRONG* decision.

Had I pulled out then, I would have possibly been able to hang on to the building and try to sell it at a loss. We could have moved out of our house of almost thirty years and tried to rent it to carry the mortgage but hang on to it.
I had pulled out the down money in the equity of our house to buy the condo/office. However, the housing market fell into the brink, and I was at least $80–$100,000 underwater on the house alone. The condo office would cost me $6,500 plus other utilities per month, and so it would continue to drag me deeper as everyone else was beginning to declare bankruptcy and most of the business offices on our block all had For Lease signs placed on them. So the hopes of renting out the building just wasn't there as well.

Like everyone else that had lost tons of money at least 40–50 percent on the market in just one day, I lost my complete retirement savings. Many who weren't in such vulnerable positions at risk in the market held on to their jobs. If they had lost some of their stock, they were able to replace it in about six months to a year after it all hit the fan. I, on the other hand, trying to save my business and my income my son's income, kept going and, without being able to borrow any more money, had to dip very deeply into my IRA account to keep our cash f low working. Still, our revenue continued to be much less than our operating expenses.
At this point with dwindling income, rising inflation, it was like everyone that had ever bought from us had left the room never to be seen again. The crushing weight is overwhelming, and for my son Jordan, as acting president and trying to manage the total demise, it became apparent that we had to let most of our

employees go, and what remained was a skeleton of what we're only a year earlier.

Employees could only call in when we had business to do. All employee morale was flushed down the drain. Our inventories were a, and yet in order to stay alive, we had to
continue to buy the necessary expensive inventory products for the printers, ink, papers, laminate, plastic parts, and cash f low our heavy shipping costs to deliver products to our remaining clients and fly our aluminum tubing and other supplies in. Even our South Korean aluminum tube manufactures could no longer give us terms, and the need for cash simply became an unmistakable impossibility.

The first of the year came around in 2011, and things were looking very bad, and we tried for a loan that at the time President Obama was promising to make $30,000 loans available to business who qualified. We totally qualified for it, but were turned down at the bank. You can imagine the huge letdown. When I heard, I was at home and I went into instant insanity over the phone. I don't even know what I said to the banker,

but finally, all of my frustration came straight out of me into the phone and I almost fainted out of complete meltdown.
That was exactly how much we needed to meet our county taxes of $29,000 for the prior year. We had until March 15 to come up with the money, and I simply did not have any more IRA money left in my retirement IRA account as they were totally exhausted. All that I had saved for my entire life was now gone. We had this

debt to pay or the business and the building would be falling into default. That is exactly what happened with literally had no way out. I realized that it has happened before many times in our country like in the '80s, where many farmers lost the farms they had had for a hundred years. The only difference is that they couldn't handle it and either tried to take revenge on the bankers and shot them or they took their own lives out of utter disgrace to themselves, their families, and their parents who couldn't face the complete horror of it all.

Although a complete tragedy had fallen upon Xtra Lite Displays® and because I was the sole owner, it came upon me and my family. I could still count on my Lord and Savior Jesus Christ who gave me and my family everything, and it was Him whom we served.

> ## *"Naked I came from my mother's womb, and naked I will depart. The Lord gave and the Lord has taken away; may the name of the Lord be praised.*
>
> *(– Job 1:21, NIV))*

This is an easy verse to remember and quote; however, it feels quite different when it happens to you for real.

I am telling you the truth that it took my wife, myself, and my family, especially Jordan's family, over three to five years to begin to heal. I personally had to read the book of Job to see how he lost everything and was accused as a sinner by all of his family and friends. His only help came from the Lord. When he faced all the tragedy around him, he gave praise to his Lord and Savior despite losing everything in his life, including his children. This picture of the depth of his losses actually makes you feel better in the lowest times of your life. That despite all that you have lost, you still own the prize of the love of God through Christ Jesus for eternity. My friend, it is the only thing that you need in this life and in the next.

I tell you these very hard and difficult things not to make you sad or talk you out of business or from reaching for the stars with your imagineering mind, but to assure you that if you are grounded in the right places to the right person, it will give you strength to forge on no matter what befalls you. Set your life and your business upon the rock of Christ, and all will be well.

## The Final Week after Fourteen Years

On April 7, 2011, after a hard-fought discussion with my brother, Al, he urged me to fold it all up. So I called Jordan and delivered the message that he had one week to close the company and find a new job. He didn't take me seriously at first, and I had to repeat it a few times. I repeated that as of Friday, we no longer exist as Xtra Lite Displays®, take all of your personal valuables and as many of the loose items as you want, and turn the lights out and lock the door. After fourteen years, we are finished.

My son Jordan, with his wisdom, immediately went about trying to find an opportunity for a new job. He knew that his future lay in his contacts and network he had developed over the last ten years as president of Xtra Lite Displays®. He reached out to one of our suppliers, a printing company in Minneapolis. He was able to establish a meeting with the president and convinced him to hire him. I found out that actually he had discussed the idea a few weeks earlier and so he knew what his decision would be. However, Jordan, being the man he is, said there was only one condition. The president asked what was that. Jordan said, *"You have to take myself and my designer, Rob, with me or I am not taking the deal."*

What he didn't know was that it was an extremely bad timing for Rob with his preemie daughter still in the NICU *(neonatal intensive care unit)*, and everything in his and his wife's world felt like it was crashing down all at once. After the initial talks with the owner of the new company that didn't point to there being a place for Rob, he was coming to terms with the idea of going freelance for a while before finding a new long-term opportunity.

The president hesitated and then flat out refused at first and Jordan replied, *"Look, the reason Xtra Lite Displays® did so well in our sales had a lot to do with our ability to design and visualize displays for our customers, so without Rob, I can't be as effective in my ability to sell for your company. So what's it going to be, me and Rob or no one?"* The president took a minute and finally realized how much Jordan needed and valued the close relationship with he and Rob and the necessity for them to function as a team. He reluctantly answered, *"Okay, then let's start you both on Monday."*

Rob said afterward he was somewhat relieved at the owner's final decision. *"I knew it would take a while, but I eventually was able to put down roots in the new company and establish myself after an emotional roller-coaster during the initial six to seven months in transition."*

Jordan did just as I had asked him and took all of his things, computers, and database of clients, and closed the doors for the last time on the Xtra Lite Display office/warehouse. Five o'clock, after all the final shipments had left, he locked the door for the very last time. I am sure there were a few tears shed because Jordan is a man of high caliber and extremely deep emotions. I love that about him; it makes him the real man that he is. On Monday of the following week, Jordan and Rob began their new jobs at their new opportunity without skipping a heartbeat. As for me, the owner and commander of the ship, as the ship takes on water and all the sailors are safely off boarded into their lifeboats, the old commander steps out onto the bow, salutes, and goes down with the ship as he exclaims…

*"Unfortunately, all of our plans in life and business are not as easy to achieve as we can foresee. The great high seas of business lurks with danger as waves roll, releasing tremendous slaps of roaring thunder against the ship's thick coat of steel, yet the hull remains intact afloat. It is the unforeseen razor tip of a mysterious iceberg that pierces through with tremendous power and unanticipated destruction. Challenging every atom of carbon once a great bastion of strength now doomed for certain failure as the crystal blades of frozen ice slice through, delivering the fatal blow and sending that once lively ship of strength to its end at the peaceful bottom."*

(–Les LaMotte • owner/commander)

*In proud and loving memory of my father, William Francis LaMotte, a WWII US Navy veteran, who served in the Harbor of the Yangtze River in Shanghai, China, in 1945-1946 as a diesel mechanic, keeping PT boat engines running, protecting the Chinese people from further Japanese aggression, and bringing about a peace on the other side of the Pacific.*

# What Form of Business Should I Consider?

## A New Business Scenario Emerges

### *Social Marketing Split Targets*

There is no longer a mono market or even a dual market; there are hundreds of splintered even undefined or underdeveloped social markets. Consider and choose your particular market, or the market segments that you feel your product serves in this multiple-market environment that exists today.

### *Brick and Mortar*

Should you consider a *"Brick and Mortar"* which comes with a heavy investment up front for buildout and high cost per square foot. Unless of course you can take something you already own or can just fix it up with low or no huge overhead or rent.

### *Mobile Hot Spots*

Consider this wisely as most businesses today are hitting the jackpot on wheels as mobile service providers, sandwich wagons, or convenient social oasis zones to serve a broader market with less up-front investment or higher investment in equipment to make their own product such as the specialty beer bars and brands.

### *Web-Based*

Or should you fall into the web hole which is absolutely easy, but the earth underneath it is shaking with changes in the general online environment, becoming watchdogs and feeling free to completely shut you down if you don't play right. It can be costly and takes a lot of time to make it fruitful. The web, even though you should have a presence today, is being used mainly for lead gathering and coupon dispensing. Statistics show that online web-store concepts are increasing because of the low price of entry, but being reduced in terms of effectiveness and quickly losing ground as it separates the customers from what they really enjoy—and that is the atmosphere, social interaction, and touch.

### Millennials

They are also generally shifting back as long as the financial markets stay at an all-time high in a demand for higher quality and are appreciating the *"hands-on homemade"* approach. They find it more fun and more exciting with more than one offering, especially those Gen-X'ers who are finally beginning a family and having to consider keeping the young ones busy, while they try to have fun like they used to.

### Gen-X

If you are specifically going for the Gen-Xer's they are actually getting very myopic. There has been some research in South Korea that reveals their eyes are changing to fit their favorite pastime, staring at their smart phones. They want speed, gaming, and just tons more of it. Their desire for things seems to be not as high unless it is faster game consoles that are more portable and function at high speed. They also tend not to participate in sports or social activities and don't need impressive clothes and things. They are not as family oriented and so aren't building for the future or long-term investments at least at this time. And who knows what that is going to look like down the road?

## Learn the Ropes of Business

### Ninety Percent of Business Is Business!

Be a student of business as much as possible. Surround yourself with people smarter than yourself who have spent more time in business. If you want to be a millionaire, hang around with millionaires. They do things differently, and you can learn what makes them successful with all the details.



Join a luncheon club like Rotary or play golf like most CEOs, and even President Trump says the best deals are made right on the greens during a nice day of golf. You learn a lot about who you may decide to do business with; you learn from them like how they respond to adversity, how they celebrate their wins, and how they treat those they hang around with.

It is extremely important to quickly get over your attachment to your product or idea. Celebrate it, develop it, then get ready to move on to being able to separate yourself from it as soon as possible. Allow it to become like another person with its own personality and its own followers. Your main goal is how to soon eclipse it with a better product because you can be sure your potential competition is out there, and they are busy working on that. If you do it, then they are left in the lurch and have to eat your dust.

Yes, to succeed you cannot fall in love with your baby. Just like farm animals whose lives are to grow up to be healthy and plump, so that they can be sold by the owner for a profit. You can't make them your beloved pets because someday they will have to give up their lives for yours. This sounds harsh, but the best business owners can do this or they will move on without the rewards of business finished well.

## Making a Business Plan

At first, I had a hard time realizing that I was in business as I was the only employee. So I had some shirts stitched with my Xtra

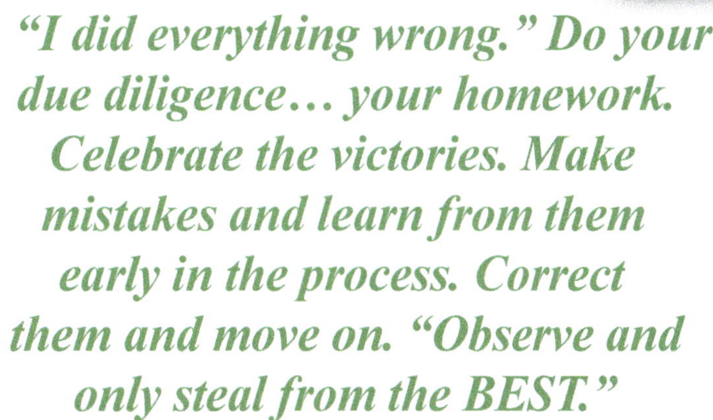

*"I did everything wrong." Do your due diligence… your homework. Celebrate the victories. Make mistakes and learn from them early in the process. Correct them and move on. "Observe and only steal from the BEST."*

*(– Les LaMotte • Imagineer)*

Lite logo on them and wore them every day. When I looked down occasionally, it helped me realize that Xtra Lite Displays was a *"real"* company and alive. Find ways to make it *"real"* for you and reinforce the good things about your product or idea in your own mind and attitude. This kind of building up will rub off on your customers and start a buzz, an excitement about your product or service. Feed and nourish it like an infant child and don't expect it to lift 200 lbs. Give it time to earn its muscle and the financial substance to do it easily.

Don't allow yourself to simply say it is too much money to start the business and then give in to what many declare is the only way to do business these days, that is, to go sell a business plan to some financial partners and ask them for all the money upfront and give up all your equity in the business to do it. If you haven't already, you need to watch a few episodes of *"Shark Tank"* and you will understand what I mean here. Many come offering only an insulting 10 percent to the Sharks and in the end have to give up sometimes as much as 51 percent because they weren't ready to understand how to do the hardest things which is SELL their product. That is what the Sharks like to see—huge numbers for the first and second year or they tell them to leave and they don't exist for them anymore.

Why do they want the big numbers? Because these guys want to come and jack up the company, grab their investment money, and take off ASAP with their gold. They aren't in business to do business. They are in business for the profit, mostly the owner's profit that the owner should have had for himself if he did not cave in to the marketing and sales options presented.

This is where most beginning companies forget: it is all about sales. *"Cash is king . . ."* It is the true picture of what your product is worth. Why not start selling your products online, then as all of the others coming into the Shark Tank, try to then get to the bigger retailers. However, they are blind as to how the big boxes work. They must give up too much, and if it doesn't sell like Walmarts, they will ship it back to you. Then you are stuck with the inventory without payment. So, go slow, sell what you can afford to make. Crawl and save until you can begin to Walk and finally when you are ready – Run. If you can do that, you will save yourself from making slimmer and slimmer margins and still holding the bag for the product and the company with all the expenses. Next thing you know, you are just one of the statistics.

Selling your product is not an evil, dirty thing to do. It is where you find out directly what your customer wants, notice I didn't say all customers. The reason is our Xtra Lite Display® customers would always ask if we made a backlit product for our XL1 displays. We would scratch our head and spend time trying to see if it were possible because of the frequency of all the requests. However, no one ever bought one and I am sure that it wasn't a real request; it was a fascination on their part. A human thing, I guess.

## Not All Customers Are Your Customers

At Xtra Lite Displays we learned the hard way that you must define and stand firm on selling your product at well above your *"breakeven"* or you loose. It is better to stand firm and loose a customer or distributor than to drag yourself in to losses on a continuous basis, while hoping for an improvement in the future.

*Not all **Customers** are **YOUR** customers
or at least permanently not your customer.
**Plant them and Pick them wisely.***
(– Les LaMotte • Imagineer)

At some place in time, they may be your best. However, over time, they can become a pain in the neck and demand lower and lower pricing which can sharply draw down your cash while you think you are making revenue with volume. Spain was one of those relationships. After several all-out fights on pricing, we cut them off and removed their distributorship. It was hard to do, but in the end, it gave us strength in the long run and we recouped.

## Success Equals - Selling Something!

Closely examine the history of recent companies, at least the small ones seek $3-million-dollar USD from angels or investors based on elaborate Business Plans. They tend to fail at alarming rates due to never figuring out that the *key to success* is not the large amount of funding money they received, but their lack of selling and monitoring their cash flow. They simply think that the stuff they have in their offices, the personnel, and the goodies they give so generously to their employees is the key to their success. However, they avoid selling the product or services like it had the plague, rather than embracing the sales part as the proof that they can succeed. Instead, they tend to have a sit back and wait attitude, and maybe squeeze another employee out of their budget that wasn't planned for or something, and get all of the right furniture and software and never spend the time to get it to make time or plans to go out and sell. So they easily give up or go back and give a sad story as to why they lost all of the investors' money and then have the absurd guts to ask for another round of money. Pretty sad. If they would only go out and start the business in a small way and experience interaction with their potential customers and their real needs first. Business is only a person with a need. You concentrate your efforts to solve the other person's need and you have begun a relationship that pays you over time. Once you have enough customers, you will feel comfortable to grow to meet the volume of needs that are required. I know you think it's boring or it's not your thing, but if you want to succeed you need to make at least 50 percent of your efforts to be in front of your customers and your income will exceed your costs.

You probably have heard that writing business plans are important, but you doubted that you could ever do it yourself and possibly it would cost a lot of your time and money to hire someone. Nothing could be farther from the truth if you use this plan developed by Bob Voss. It is a one-of-a-kind approach, and by using it he has earned the approval of his bankers, angel investors, and raised over six million in startup capital, using these simple principles it will get you off to a fast start on the right foot. It is important to first prove to your investors that you know your business. Yes, you can get help along the way, but that is what I or Bob can help you with. On the following page (139) is an outline that takes you through the entire twenty-one steps of doing a business plan. It is well worth putting sometime into this task. It will help you realize whether you have a Business or how far you would have to modify your Business idea before it would make true Business sense to proceed. Some Business Ideas are just that ideas that maybe or for your good and your investors should not be invested in. Applying this Due Diligence and discipline will prevent you from entering into a disaster and complete loss or a complete success with your investment.

## Taking the Mystery Out of Creating a Brilliant Business or Non-profit Plan

To easily create your own plan for each of your business or non-profit ideas, just answer the following twenty-one questions.

# 21 Question ~~Business~~ *Confidence* Plan™

## Part 1: You and Your Business or Non-Profit Idea

1. How would you describe your business or non-profit idea?
2. Why are you starting this business or non-profit venture?
3. Why are you the right person to start, run, and own this business or non-profit?
4. How is your business or non-profit organized?
5. What goals do you want to accomplish in the first twelve months of your business or non-profit?

## Part 2: Research, Competition, and Competitive Advantages

6. Why is this business or non-profit a good business or non-profit to start?
7. Who is your competition?
8. What are your competitive advantages?

## Part 3: Sales, Prices, and Margins

9. How much do you charge for your products or services?
10. What is the reasoning behind your prices?
11. How much do you make on what you sell?
12. What do you estimate your first year sales will be by month?

## Part 4: Getting Known by Your Target Customers

13. How would you describe your target customers?
14. What marketing tactics are you going to use to get known by your target customers?
15. When people see your marketing materials (website, brochures, ads, etc.), what messages do you want them to remember?
16. What are you going to do on a very regular basis to constantly and consistently get new customers?

## Part 5: Financials

17. What are your start-up costs?
18. What is your monthly overhead?
19. How many sales do you need on a monthly basis to break even?
20. What are the highlights of your first year projections?

## Part 6: The Last Question

21. What *Proof* do you have that this business or non-profit is going to succeed?

Download the full worksheet with explanations for each question.

*Created by Robert Voss © 2017 Bizowner Training LLC • BizownerTraining.com*

**17**

*What Form of Business Should I Consider?*

## Be Patient

*Crawl – Walk – Run & Fly*. Slow down and really think it through first. Don't expect it all overnight. Reserve some cash from the *"good days"*. Make calculated changes in your life and in your business pursuits. When I finally felt the accolades of others for what I had accomplished in a short time, I reminded them and declared that I was an *"overnight success"* that took thirty-five years in the making.

## Select or Create… the Right Company Model

What is the general business size, legal entity, purpose and life expectancy? These are all basic questions you have to wrestle with if you are going decide the right form and fit for your company or service to permit growth and last over time. Wow, I didn't realize that you can choose the form that best fits your business or that there were many ways to form a business. Yes, there are about as many as there are businesses.
*Put on your Imagineering cap and get a pencil to create yours!*

## Marketing as a Shell Company

Doing business as a shell company that does the marketing and relies on outside providers or shippers to fulfill your business can be a very risky way to build a business. You are asking others to be as diligent as you would be with your products, your clients, your profit, and your general control of quality—and all of these factors can spin out of control in no time leaving you with a real mess and upset customers, that will not be coming back anytime too soon.

**Figure 4**

$$Q = SQRT((2*D*S)/h)$$

|   | 30 | 36 | 48 |
|---|---|---|---|
| D = | 131 | 442 | 84 |
| S = | $495.00 | $495.00 | $495.00 |
| h = | 10 | 10 | 10 |
| Q = | 114 | 209 | 91 |

| Rollup Sales per Quarter | | | | | |
|---|---|---|---|---|---|
| **Figure 1** | | | Rollup sizes | | |
| | | | 30" | 36" | 48" |
| 2005 | 1st Qtr | Jan - Mar | 66 | 43 | 7 |
| | 2nd Qtr | Apr - Jun | 26 | 30 | 17 |
| | 3rd Qtr | Jul - Sep | 39 | 280 | 21 |
| | 4th Qtr | Oct - Dec | 22 | 121 | 23 |
| 2006 | 1st Qtr | Jan - Mar | 21 | 54 | 33 |
| | 2nd Qtr | Apr - Jun | 15 | 100 | 12 |
| | 3rd Qtr | Jul - Sep | 48 | 71 | 12 |
| | 4th Qtr | Oct - Dec | 23 | 147 | 12 |
| 2007 | 1st Qtr | Jan - Mar | 42 | 82 | 15 |
| | 2nd Qtr | Apr - Jun | 32 | 193 | 10 |
| | 3rd Qtr | Jul - Sep | 27 | 94 | 68 |
| | Total Demand | | 361 | 1215 | 230 |
| | Avg Demand per year | | 131.27 | 441.82 | 83.64 |
| | Mean | | 32.82 | 110.45 | 20.91 |
| | SD | | 14.85 | 73.46 | 17.23 |

$ TM Math Model for Purchasing FREE @ LesLaMotte.com

## Refine Your Purchasing to Your Advantage

We first found and sold our unique small plastic map cases with Alvin company, an art supplier on the East Coast. We would continually look at our product price make up, and we like any company wanted to lower our overhead and make sure we had a ready access to our base products for quick orders. With Alvin, whom we purchased the cases from initially, it was a problem of attitude. To them they were just selling something they sold. We found out all too soon that they were out until the next shipment from overseas which left us without the ability to sell our product at all.

We simply couldn't operate effectively this way. So we asked them to come to a new arrangement where they purchase the cases from us at a set price. At first they were reluctant but, then they realized that a cooperative approach might work better. We made an agreement with them. If they gave us the name of the manufacturer, we would inventory the product for them and give them greater access to the product at a set price, but increased the colors available and an add-on additional larger product we would develop with the same manufacturing company in Italy. They thought it over and agreed and then begin ordering from us, thus, removing their need to be involved with the nuisance of shipping overseas for this particular product, therefore, giving them an advantage of price and availability as well. Also, we gained the advantage of having them on hand when we needed them. When we needed to order, we would call them and ask if they needed additional inventory. In the end, both of us got what we were looking for. Therefore, we were able to make a difficult relationship work to both of our advantages.

# Wood Chopping Your Business Plan

## Taking the First Steps Seriously

Considering that all businesses need a huge dose of passion to begin with, but, to move forward, passion is not the only quality that builds and sustains them. You must endure and triumph over a huge dose of business planning. Do as much as you can before attempting to begin.

Take the time to know your numbers down to the cents because in business, even cents can make a difference. It is not about what most young business owners are told, that you go do a huge business plan that will "blow the socks off your financial angels." You get their $3 million dollars and float off into the sunset as a multi-millionaire. Some of the biggest mistakes are made by business launches that are based on fancy spreadsheets that they know are irresponsible and highly subjective without a shred of evidence that their model will work. Normally, these kinds of business will go out and spend from their known amount of budgets and spend it all end up with no reserves and fail in about one to two years. Notoriously going back to the well for another infusion of money, lots of money.

1. Ask yourself, and I mean sincerely, are you the first one to have offered such a  product or service in this particular market. If not, who else is in your space? In the US? In other countries?

2. Why is your product or service so superior or what does it do that the competitors could not even address or seem to understand about the consumers' needs that yours totally fulfills?

3. What is the highest price point your customer will purchase at and lowest you can afford to produce your product? The profit spread.

4. Rule of Thumb Price Setting Model: At what price point can you market it at that will reflect your customers' comfort zone?

5. How long will you be able to stay at that price point before your competition begins to change their product to match or exceed your design/service or lower their price in the market place?

Realistically today, it could be only days or weeks—with the advent of Chinese and Asian partners and others, depending on your product manufacturing methods—the speed by which they can re-engineer *(tear yours apart)*, engineer a better alternative, mold, create electronic circuit board designs, make it, package and ship it, and ***enact changes, is simply mind bogglingly fast.*** Then send it for mass production and marketing on Amazon in a few minutes, then it is on your doorstep in only a few weeks.

## How Xtra Lite Displays Started Out With a Bang

I simply built my Xtra Lite business on the fact that I had no money. What I did have was a fantastic product, and what I absolutely needed now was the sales of this fantastic product. I just spent a small amount to go to trade shows and showing the upgrades to my product until it was fully realized. The end result was sales.

One of my first was for a Christian company that worked in Bible translation. John, a former young missionary and indirectly a relative, who just came back with his wife and family from Africa, was in need of employment. So I shared with him my new display product and offered him a sales opportunity—not a job as I wasn't quite ready for that just yet. As a great missionary who was used to talking and sharing with people, he set out to find missionary companies who needed extremely light portable displays. He knew many Christian mission groups and just sat down and called on them. One of his first contacts was with a Wycliffe Bible translators. The company expressed their need for three hundred displays for their translators to use in promoting their work in churches building their support for their next years mission work.

Wow, what a boom! John got the order and after we had it in hand, I thought about what I now needed to do. I received their artwork and proceeded to find a good large-scale digital printer as they were quite new at the time in the late nineties. We had a sample printed and made the correct sized display and sent it to them for their approval. They called and said enthusiastically that they loved it. I gave them the final invoice and then asked if they could send me 50 percent of the order up front. The next day I received a wire for $85,000, the entire amount to my bank account. I sat down and took my breath. I finally realized for the first time that I was now in business. I had not only an order but a huge order with the funds to carry it through. It finally struck me that I was really in business.

## Product / Service Business Budgeting

This took me by surprise when I first learned how to predict and keep track of my small business income to make money, not lose it.

## Formula for Calculating Your Business Revenue
## to Target Your Gross *"Required for Success"* Earnings Per Year

**$ Start Here**

*Record all of your personal financial needs per year.*

*Example:*

**X3**

### Your Income Needed

| | | |
|---|---|---|
| **Personal $ Need** | $ | 65,000 |
| **Plus 10% Savings** | $ | 6,500 |
| **Total Personal** | $ | 71,500 |

x **3** = $ 214,500

### Total Business Revenue Needed

| | |
|---|---|
| $ 214,500 | Total Business Revenue Needed per Year |
| $ 735 | / **292** = Business Revenue per Day (5 Days / Wk) |
| $ 4,125 | / **52** = Business Revenue per Week |
| $ 17,875 | / **12** = Business Revenue per Month |
| $ 53,625 | / **4** = Business Revenue per Quarter |

**Cash Flow Checker**

## Try Yours Here

| | | |
|---|---|---|
| **Personal $ Need** | $ | |
| **Plus 10% Savings** | $ | |
| **Total Personal** | $ | |

x **3** = $

### Total Business Revenue Needed

| | |
|---|---|
| $ | Total Business Revenue Needed per Year |
| $ | / **292** = Business Revenue per Day (5 Days / Wk) |
| $ | / **52** = Business Revenue per Week |
| $ | / **12** = Business Revenue per Month |
| $ | / **4** = Business Revenue per Quarter |

> *"Some 20% of small businesses fail in their first year, 30% of small businesses fail in their second year, and 50% of small businesses fail after five years in business. Finally, 30% of small-business owners fail in their tenth year in business."*

*Last Update: August 6, 2018 https://www.fundera.com/blog/what-percentage-of-small-businesses-fail*



Now, take your total amount of revenue for your budget categories and divide them out over twelve months. Then adjust the amounts for the windfall months and the dry months so that in the end, you will have an idea of exactly how much you need for each month in reserve.

You then keep track of the income each week, month, quarter, and adjust your plan as the year progresses. Always make sure you are hitting your numbers. If one month makes more than you figured then simply add it to the reserves of the next month. Keep moving the income and debt to the next month until you can predict your outcome for the year. If you do it well, then keep this record for the next year and adjust the amounts based on prior year real revenues.

> *"Let me reassure you that once I figured this out, I began to make money."*

*(– Les LaMotte • Imagineer)*

So where does the other two-thirds of the revenue go and how is it used? You have to consider yourself as one of the costs. The other one-third is the *"cost of doing business"*—the inventory, the machines, the paper clips, etc. The final one-third is that one that normally escapes you… if you make money, you need to send it in. Yes, the last third provides the *various taxes, personal, business, and sales tax*.

## It Always Costs More Than You Think

The killer of all good business is the costs you never realized. These are the hidden costs, which are the variable ones, that will take you back negatively and impact to *slow down your business growth and potential.* The insurance usually costs way more than you are prepared for, and it is based on assets and revenue so it changes over time if you are growing so does it. All of your business costs including sales inventory, general upkeep costs, employee costs, and the insurance man just takes a higher percentage and wishes you well for the next great sales your you will have. Maddening you do the excellent job of increasing your income and they say thank you we will take our part now as well. Another cost is security.  If you have a building filled with assets naturally you would want security to protect your employees, inventory, and machines or paperwork that keeps growing.

These days it is all about the medical insurance and incentives for your employees as they expect and want you to provide a much higher level of benefits than employers did ten or twenty years ago.

The Internet has become a huge cost for both the service, the cost of keeping your employees on target and on the job and as the computer boosts your creativity it silently steels away employee time.

HR is one that creeps up on you, and today it is a huge part of running any business. Hiring and firing could not be any more costly or touchy and downright difficult to do it right or pay the price for many years to come without their specific legal eye on the game for you giving you advice that could save you thousands.

### Product or Service Pricing Strategy

This took me by surprise when I first learned of how the pricing strategy is so important to establish right up front. Common knowledge, if that is what you have come to rely on to gauge how you could make money with your product or service, it is not a good teacher here and *it is the reason most small business fail and fail fast!*

What if you are going to sell through multi-levels of marketing and distributors? In order for you to price your product for that kind of business venture, you have to use one of the following schemes.

### Craft Fairs or On-Off Pricing Scheme: 2x's Mark-up

This is the way to market small products at fairs and small business. Make an Excel sheet that includes all of your costs, the cost of your final product with all of the cost included, shipping, labor, overhead, total cost of product, and tooling and then mark-up them up three times. The resulting price will probably shock you from a consumer's perspective. Now, if and only if you can sell your present product manufactured the way you can presently do it with all of these revealed costs included, you can begin selling it. I would surely add an additional 10 percent at the bottom for contingencies that may incur.

### Online Sales Pricing Scheme: 3x's – 5x's Mark-up

The next step in a pricing scheme is for small companies selling online or in a one-shop boutique environment, and you are the only seller of the product. You are not selling to Target or other big box retailers at this time.

Taking into consideration everything above, you must consider one more factor: how long should the product sit on the shelf before it turns to cash in your business account. To make sure to avoid losing money, you need to consider a five times markup. Product Turn-over is very important consideration here. The large box stores like Walmart keep watch hourly, daily, and weekly. If a product doesn't turn fast enough they either don't order it again or they slow their purchasing of it.

Yes, after all of the costs plus that 10 percent of unknown and the result is the starting retail price. After you know that number, now consider your market place. Now put a number you would pay for it in the market. Okay, now compare. Do you have it right or are you too high or too low? There are various other marketing tips to price selling and that is to round up the price and then remove a few cents to make it fit a particular *"customer norm"*. Why is it that everything in the store or online is not $10 but, rather $9.95 or the new $9.97? You guessed it, the customer only sees the first number, and they don't recognize or consider the change in their buying decision.

### Big Box Retail Pricing Scheme – 10x's Mark-up

The most familiar to larger product companies is pricing based on the *"suggested retail price,"* the general concept of which is that other large box stores (and you have to check their actual policies for suggested retail pricing), they expect at least a minimum of 50 percent or a *"keynote."* So you must be able to sell it to them with all of your costs including shipping, taxes, and insurance to their door for 50 percent of your suggested retail price. Now, they are not obligated to sell it at the suggested retail price and may see it as a *"lost leader"* to get people into the store. Your overall pricing scheme must allow for you or your other distributors to still make the same markup even if you get a Big Box store selling at under your retail pricing.

This then requires a projected markup of at least eight to ten times to achieve a profitable venture. A long way from where you thought you could undercut everyone in the market place now isn't it! But it is absolutely the way business works, and so you must live within the system to sell into Big box retailers. You may or may not be able to base on the consumers' price consideration for your product.

Never give your product away as a prize or raffle. That will cheapen the value of your product in your potential customers' eyes and give it a negative mind share.
Never drop or discount your products all the time. You may for a short season do so to put that spin on their mind share, but possibly by the time they get to buying, it will no longer be available at the discounted price. To save face with their boss, their need, themselves, and possibly their friends, they will just buy it anyway at the full price. That short discount-time period with specific times of start and finish can put your product on their top-of-mind awareness as they add up the reasons why they need your product.

If you make the mistake of trying to move your product into a market at a low price, you are doomed before you begin. First of all, if your product is introduced at a low price, then you must explain that it is Only a *"Limited Time Offer"*. In other words, buy it now or you will have to pay at full price down the road. The rule of thumb is that consumers remember your product and price as a unit. If you introduce it without fair warnings that it won't be there long at that price, you will be forever stuck with that reduced price, and the customers will demand further discounts. You never want to sell a product at a loss. What is the point? The only companies who do this as a strategy to purchase the entire consumer base and put their competition out of business in this particular category or product. It is costly, but, it does destroy the other product which rarely recovers.

You never want to knowingly give away or discount your product directly. You want to bundle it with something of lesser value so that in the end, the consumer still pays full retail for your product and you gave away some other cheap item to take advantage of their tendency for buying anything that says *"Sale"* on it. The way to anticipate this is to determine how many you can give away or at a reduced price to get the consumers hooked on your product, and driving their family and friends to go and get your wonderful product in the stores. That is simply accomplished by coupons or two for one or other marketing tricks and gimmicks to get them hooked on your product. Ever notice how many products are advertised for a huge discount, but when you go to the store to pick it up, the advertising date is no longer valid. What do you do? Normally, since you are already there, you buy it anyway.

## Advertising and Marketing Strategy

It is said by advertising companies that your advertising budget no matter how much you can muster will only be worth 50 percent of the results. That is rather low and most believe today that advertising, unless it is on the Internet and social media, is just a waste of money altogether. How will you deal with that reality in your planning to achieve much more for every dollar you spend? Marketing in my day amounted to mailed cards, fliers, and brochures. Today, sophisticated social media composite segments working together can accomplish a great deal, but depending on your market and whether that market share is computer savvy, you cannot reach them that efficiently.

*So what are the alternatives?* Back when Xtra Lite Displays® was doing well we used post cards that were sent out to mega thousands of potential leads. At best you were told that if you get 1-1.5 percent, you were really doing well. We did okay and we did it for many years with only minor success, but it did one thing—gave us leads that we then owned and could send to again and again.

We found that the best way to advertise was to use your product *as cash* to purchase costly services of print advertising in market and business magazines. This practice did give us some clout after a while as everyone knew who we were and when we saw them at local trade shows they would come and visit us to see what was new. As far as leads we took, they were limited if I remember correctly, but, whatever we received went into our main database.

At that same time, many companies were trying to find other companies with similar advertising and marketing that they could work together and share the load as long as off slightly. they were not direct competitors. You still see this sometimes today but, it has dropped Tod y's market is all about the element of surprise and juxtaposition of your product, so that it stands out in the way it is being used or how to associate nature or animals with it so that the audience is drawn into watching, and then some erroneous transformation to your product. To me, as a designer, these lack the direct approach altogether in exchange for the entertainment factor which I am not sure it is always successful. Well, I hope it is working for them. It is best used by advertisers of the Super Bowl with an inflated viewer base and spending millions on high end production values. Not for beginners in the market place for sure.

## Patents, Trademarks, and Other Legal Tools

Is a patent important? Or are there other faster means to bring your product or service to the market more affordably and at the same time will give you some legal control? Let me save you an easy $25,000 to $100,000 and let you know that No, there are other options.

Filing a full patent will, first, cost you a lot of money. Second, it will take about two years and slow down the release of your product for sales. Third, defending a patent today will cost you $250,000 up front just to get it to Federal Court to defend it. Most small businesses have no business even considering a full patent. Fourth, what good are they? In my case the only thing I can say that it did for me in my fourteen years is possibly keep many other companies from wanting to get involved in legal costs and entanglement.

Today, you can file your own Design Patent, which gives you some basis for trying to keep people from copying your product for a while and maybe long enough. So you use the principle of eclipsing your own product, which is making the next generation that is bigger and better, so they can't just knock you off. You become your own competitor. Therefore, you avoid that whole costly issue. The only caution is if you are creating medical hardware and software, then all bets are off, and you have to file a normal full patent. Why, because the real dirty secret is that 95 percent of all patents are for medical hardware and software industries who have the attorney's and the high income ratios to afford them.

***DON'T GET SOLD A BILL OF GOODs** from a slick patent peddler they are completely worthless and it will cost you plenty with no or limited results!*

Consider, another layer of approach in trademarking your product name or service. This will allow you to go to market faster and at a fraction of the cost as you can do it yourself for a few hundred dollars. Trademarks are good for two reasons. Customers *"Top Head Memory"* of your name is your most important asset. Having a US trademark gives you an easy way to catch other mimicking your product name or logo and is far easier to legally file cease and desist letters and collect for illegally using your trademark for their gain. It can also help keep other similar products out of the US, and you can go to court immediately without any great investment or make a cash deal with the other company. You can immediately put legal pressure on the other party in the US or outside the US for infringing on your trademarked logo and /or your trademarked name. They each are separate entities and can be trademarked separately and defended as two issues. The *"Common Law"* states that you simply add a *"™"* on each aspect of your name and your logo/logotype. That gives you one year from the date it hits the streets to file for the actual trademark. This includes all inventions, written, and artistic work or photography.

## Establishing First Art

In most patent, name, or trademark issues, the best policy to protect them is first sketch them *(not paste)* your idea in a bound volume *(one with a hard spine)* with written detail on what it is and why and how it works. Then have someone you trust review the idea in the book and sign and date their name in the book—this is what is referred to as *"First Art."* This is a must before you apply for a patent, name, logo/logotype, and trademark especially for filing a worldwide patent.

The next thing is that you need to display each item you wish to trademark on an 8.5"x11" sheet in black and white only, without the "™" in place. This along with the written trademark forms found on line at the patent and trademark website, and your check and mail them in. You are done, good job on your first and least expensive offense of your valued product or service!

## Your Mission Statement

Make sure you can write down or explain your entire business plan on a napkin or it probably is not a workable plan at all. If you can't, then first, it must be way too complex and needs to be simplified and condensed. This is necessary because you will have to share your business with those around you including others in your company, your bankers, your angel, or your employees.

Never go into business without a complete business plan that includes extensive knowledge and research on these three major factors: finance, product / service, and marketing resources.

## A Word of Caution

When you begin your business, you will quickly see that all of your expectations and careful planning will have to change. You will realize all too quickly that the plan is just that, a plan. Carrying out the plan is another concept altogether. You will be tweaking the plan continuously as the plan is nothing more than a beginning base in which to prove whether it is true or that it needs constant adjustment. As the business plan changes, you need to adjust your baseline assumptions as well to update your initial assumptions and align the direction of your business. In fact in the beginning you need to keep very closed to keeping track of all numbers each week and make adjustments as needed ASAP and keep good records so you can begin to forecast in about six months to a year.

If you find out that you have totally underestimated your costs to produce and market your product, you may have to consider removing it from the market at your expense and revamping the branding and later reintroduce it with a new packaging, bottle, shape, benefits at a higher price, in order to resume in that particular market.

Don't go overboard on making your marketing plan. It is best that YOU attempt it even though you don't feel totally comfortable. Your potential partners or funders will want to be reassured that you first, can write a plan to include all of the base numbers and see the percentages of your start up money will be spent in the right way as to grow your business quickly. Second, that you understand your business throughly enough to be able to foresee many of the possible challenges in such a plan. By doing this, you will soon learn all of the real costs of your product and begin to consider if it is worthy of the market or if you have to revamp your basic ideas. Resist the modern tendency today to try to initially remove all the possible leaks and fall prey to quickly turning it over to a so-called expert or high-priced accountant or CPA. Stop and think, what do they really know about anything you are doing? After all, were you not the one who came up with the basic ideas? How could they completely understand the expertise you specifically have already exhibited to come up with the idea to begin with? Developing muscles for your health is good. Here, it is also healthy to build your business muscles to get to the first stage of your business. Simply get an online free business plan spreadsheet and begin to fill in what you know and research the things that you have no idea about. But, wrestle with the complete Business Buster issues *NOW BEFORE* you begin.

Like in getting offices and spending large sums of money, wait, reposition, wait, reposition at least four times. Then start to gather specific actual sales and sales and marketing from your initial plan before or if you determine that it is out of your league. Subsequently, look for bright but not too expensive professional accountants and part-time business managers for some advice on your record keeping and determine if their help could benefit your present state of business. As you see growth, you will need to hire a part-time or full-time professional. Keep checking your assumptions against actual sales and cost data recording and reviewing them often probably daily for the first six months of operations. Prove to yourself that your assumptions line up with the reality and if not, recalibrate so that you can determine your *"break-even"* position each week, month, and year so you can make accurate predictions and restocking purchases in a very understandable and smooth process.

***Rule of thumb:*** You are the visionary; the one driving the car looking through the front window, steering where and how you are going toward your goal. Your accountants and CPAs are fixated on the rearview mirror and keeping good records of where you have been. The MBA or other professionals are there as tools for you to use as necessary, not the ones who are in control of your destiny. Make your own choices and live with them. Just know that when you steer that car wheel, know where you are going and how much it will cost you to go there and establish the speed and fuel usage according to your ability to sell your product or services.

A good alternative today is online sites that pace you through and guide you as you do the *"driving"*. Spit out the needed paperwork that allows you to visualize the cash flow and break-even points to make immediate and important decisions before they cause problems. Find something that is good enough such as some reasonable software or online service that you can understand and has a proven track record of good results.

## Efficacy and Market Reachability

Know your market expectations, the costs of your competitors, the cost of marketing, and either find a way to do it better or for less money or you will not stand a chance against a large competitor. Find out the actual possible number of customers you can support or reach with your product or service. Don't be a high school kid and think that you can reach 10 percent of the country. While it is good to look at that fantasy revenue, let's break it down to your city, your state, the US, and each country in the world that may need or want what you have to offer.

Now, put three numbers down: the crawl amount, the walk amount, the run amount and the fly amount which is really your sales amount after 5 years in your business. These may represent one-year segments or a number of years or just in a month's time. Now, build the market share slowly starting at 1–3 percent and on up. Chances are even if you give it your complete all, you will probably never meet anything more than 10 percent of any one particular market segment you try for. Build into your marketing plan allowing for 5–10 percent of your overall budget to be used as your marketing budget.

*Market Share* represents the percentage of an industry or market's total sales that is earned by a particular company over a specific time period. Market share is calculated by taking the company's sales over the period and dividing it by the total sales of the entire industry over the same period. *(https://www.investopedia.com/terms/m/marketshare.asp)*

Website strategies today include driving the crowd or *"traffic"* to your website, so they can then download coupons or see offers that will entice them to bite or take action toward your product or services. It is kind of a hunt for the best options, so they experience and therefore believe that they have done everything they could to get their best deal so they can act on it.

Provide them with a good reason to go to your website. If you have multiple products, provide a special landing page so that they can choose from your offerings. This way, you can grow your mailing list organically from hot prospects. This is also a good way to qualify them as to their interest and the exact kind of interest that they have so you can develop submarket offers and deliver them to pre-qualified and narrow your liability to a large-scale offering for large discounts, free products etc.

As a former trade show company, I don't want you to forget about trade shows; however, make sure you are targeting your actual audience who want your specific product. Otherwise, you can spend your way without a single lead in ROI. There are a few things to consider when trying to figure out which tradeshow is right for your product or service.

Try not to just give in easily to your industry trade show that everyone else goes to time after time, and it is an old boys' or girls' club. I can assure you, you can't sell to your competitors and why inform them of your sales offers or tactics anyway. Chances are that you will just be seen as just another option without distinction.
Try to find new or smaller shows and consider spending less on each show and do more shows. Remember 80 percent is just showing up and a much better opportunity if you are the only one of your kind present. In this kind of a scenario, you have a much better chance at speaking with potential customers with more intensity regarding their interest.

Pick your shows very wisely and consider going to a new show for the first year just to walk the show to see or report back to you who and what is happening, and then you can make an educated strategic plan for the following year or skip it altogether. Being fully prepared with the right materials and presentation is very important. Remember you are fishing… and the fish does not always take the bait that you are offering. But if you find out their preferred bait and presentation, then get ready to pull them in fast and fill the boat.

## How to Figure Out the ROI *(Return on Investment)* for Trade Shows

This is the quick formula to figure out your potential ROI per trade show you wish to attend. You can make a simple spreadsheet and do a quick analysis of each show to determine the best shows to attend.

- What is the total Universe of attendees for the particular show, *For example:* 20,000 attendees.

- Multiply that number by approximately 17–19 percent. This will give you the approximate number of potential buyers at the show who might be interested in your product or service. *For example:* 18 percent of the total number of attendees would be 3,600 potentially interested people.

- Divide the number of potential customers you could talk to by the hours of the show. *For example:* 3,600 attendees divided by 5 hours = 720 attendees per hour to speak to.

- How much time does it take to explain your product or average conversation you will need? *For example:* 5 minutes divided by 3,600 attendees by 5 hours = 2.4 personnel are needed in your booth in order to capture and explain the product's benefit to all of your potential customers at this particular show.

- Out of those, you have about a 3-5 percent chance *(you will start with this and then refine as you go to shows)* at converting attendees into customers. *For example:* 3,600 attendees / 5 percent = 180 conversions.

- Take all of the costs related to going to that show and put them on a spreadsheet. *For example:* $10,000 - total show expenditures including personnel and travel / 180 potential conversions = $55.55 cost per converted lead.

- The total of actual business generated by the show = $75,000; less the cost of attending the show of $10,000 = $65,000 / $55.55. You will have a gain of $1,170 per lead ROI after all expenses.

## Keeping Your Eyes on the Numbers

### Make Sure You Are Tracking Them Weekly / Monthly / Yearly

## COGS (Cost of Goods Sold)

| | Jan | Feb | Mar | Apr | May | Jun | Jul | Aug | Sep | Oct | Nov | Dec | Total |
|---|---|---|---|---|---|---|---|---|---|---|---|---|---|
| Sales: | 95,278 | 73,281 | 108,421 | 78,406 | 100,043 | 114,670 | 83,978 | 151,182 | 114,312 | 96,909 | 73,274 | 93,671 | 1,183,425 |
| COGS: | | | | | | | | | | | | | |
| Raw Materials | 22,390 | 17,221 | 25,479 | 18,425 | 23,510 | 26,947 | 19,735 | 35,528 | 26,863 | 22,774 | 17,219 | 22,013 | 278,104 |
| Wages | 9,433 | 7,255 | 10,734 | 7,762 | 9,904 | 11,352 | 8,314 | 14,967 | 11,317 | 9,594 | 7,254 | 9,273 | 117,159 |
| Freight In | 3,906 | 3,005 | 4,445 | 3,215 | 4,102 | 4,701 | 3,443 | 6,198 | 4,687 | 3,973 | 3,004 | 3,841 | 48,520 |
| Freight Out | 4,097 | 3,151 | 4,662 | 3,371 | 4,302 | 4,931 | 3,611 | 6,501 | 4,915 | 4,167 | 3,151 | 4,028 | 50,887 |
| Misc | 762 | 586 | 867 | 627 | 800 | 917 | 672 | 1,209 | 914 | 775 | 586 | 749 | 9,464 |
| Total COGS | 40,588 | 31,218 | 46,187 | 33,400 | 42,618 | 48,848 | 35,775 | 64,403 | 48,696 | 41,283 | 31,214 | 39,904 | 504,134 |
| Gross Profit | 54,690 | 42,063 | 62,234 | 45,006 | 57,425 | 65,822 | 48,203 | 86,779 | 65,616 | 55,626 | 42,060 | 53,767 | 679,291 |
| EXPENSES: | | | | | | | | | | | | | |
| Personnel | 18,960 | 14,583 | 21,576 | 15,603 | 19,909 | 22,819 | 16,712 | 30,085 | 22,748 | 19,285 | 14,582 | 18,641 | 235,503 |
| Building/Lease | 8,003 | 6,156 | 9,107 | 6,586 | 8,404 | 9,632 | 7,054 | 12,699 | 9,602 | 8,140 | 6,155 | 7,868 | 99,406 |
| Promotion (Sales Rep) | 8,099 | 6,229 | 9,216 | 6,665 | 8,504 | 9,747 | 7,138 | 12,850 | 9,717 | 8,237 | 6,228 | 7,962 | 100,592 |
| Communications | 2,191 | 1,685 | 2,494 | 1,803 | 2,301 | 2,637 | 1,931 | 3,477 | 2,629 | 2,229 | 1,685 | 2,154 | 27,216 |
| Xerox | 858 | 660 | 976 | 706 | 900 | 1,032 | 756 | 1,361 | 1,029 | 872 | 659 | 843 | 10,652 |
| Product Development | 667 | 513 | 759 | 549 | 700 | 803 | 588 | 1,058 | 800 | 678 | 513 | 656 | 8,284 |
| All Other | 6,193 | 4,763 | 7,047 | 5,096 | 6,503 | 7,454 | 5,459 | 9,827 | 7,430 | 6,299 | 4,763 | 6,089 | 76,923 |
| Total Expenses | 44,971 | 34,589 | 51,175 | 37,008 | 47,221 | 54,124 | 39,638 | 71,357 | 53,955 | 45,740 | 34,585 | 44,213 | 558,576 |
| Net Ordinary Income | 9,719 | 7,474 | 11,059 | 7,998 | 10,204 | 11,698 | 8,565 | 15,422 | 11,661 | 9,886 | 7,475 | 9,554 | 120,715 |
| Interest Expense | 1,048 | 806 | 1,193 | 862 | 1,100 | 1,261 | 924 | 1,663 | 1,257 | 1,066 | 806 | 1,030 | 13,016 |
| Net Income | 8,671 | 6,668 | 9,866 | 7,136 | 9,104 | 10,437 | 7,641 | 13,759 | 10,404 | 8,820 | 6,669 | 8,524 | 107,699 |
| Sales | 95,278 | 73,281 | 108,421 | 78,406 | 100,043 | 114,670 | 83,978 | 151,182 | 114,312 | 96,909 | 73,274 | 93,671 | 1,183,425 |
| Net Income | 8,671 | 6,668 | 9,866 | 7,136 | 9,194 | 10,437 | 7,641 | 13,759 | 10,404 | 8,820 | 6,669 | 8,524 | 107,699 |
| % Income vs Gross | 9.10% | 9.10% | 9.10% | 9.10% | 9.19% | 9.10% | 9.10% | 9.10% | 9.10% | 9.10% | 9.10% | 9.10% | 9.10% |

| Xtra Lite Display Systems Inc | | | | | | | | | | | | | |
|---|---|---|---|---|---|---|---|---|---|---|---|---|---|
| Non- Profit Sales | | | | | | | | | | | | | |
| 3 Yr Average | | | | | | | | | | | | | |
| Year | Jan | Feb | Mar | Apr | May | Jun | Jul | Aug | Sep | Oct | Nov | Dec | Total |
| 2000 | 706 | 122 | 1,895 | 1,258 | 4,566 | 9,219 | 2,393 | 3,466 | 13,205 | 4,114 | 2,186 | 6,335 | 49,465 |
| 2001 | 19,611 | 3,389 | 7,558 | 6,983 | 6,705 | 5,319 | 9,471 | 18,820 | 5,209 | 9,500 | 4,281 | 928 | 97,774 |
| 2002 | 17,143 | 5,762 | 2,488 | 1,775 | 5,336 | 4,424 | 4,361 | 4,264 | 10,576 | 7,427 | 9,955 | 1,728 | 75,239 |
| Avg | 12,487 | 3,091 | 3,980 | 3,339 | 5,536 | 6,321 | 5,408 | 8,850 | 9,663 | 7,014 | 5,474 | 2,997 | 74,159 |

## Make Sure You Are Understanding Your Monthly Averages to Project Future Performance

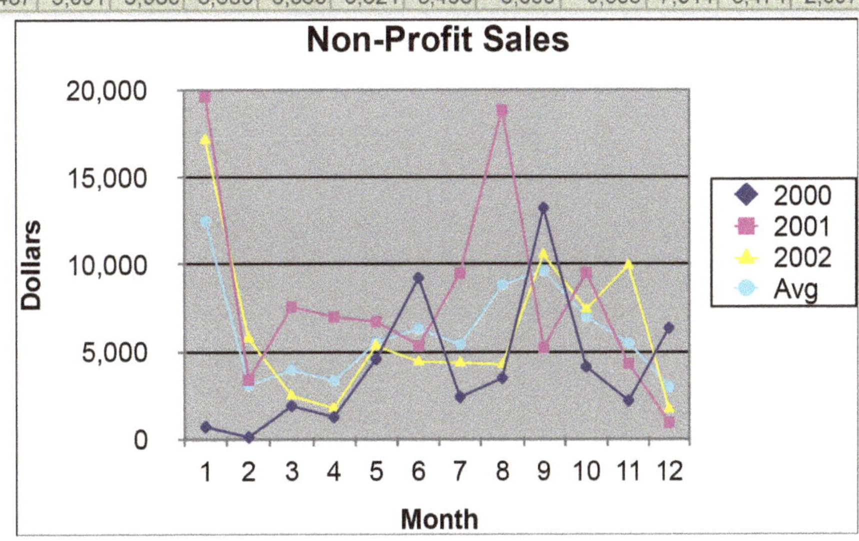



*Wood Chopping Your Business Plan*     19

| Xtra Lite Displays | | |
|---|---|---|
| **Overhead Rate** | **2004** | **2005** |
| **Expenses:** | | |
| Cost of Goods Sold | 343,824 | 255,511 |
| Expenses | 461,448 | 311,050 |
| Interest | 11,995 | 7,540 |
| **Total** | **$817,267** | **$574,101** |
| | | |
| **Less Directly Recovered Expenses:** | | |
| Freight Out | 33,795 | 24,437 |
| Cost of Materials | 188,222 | 151,268 |
| **Total** | **$222,017** | **$175,705** |
| | | |
| **Other Expenses:** | | |
| Non-Billable Expenses | 595,250 | 398,396 |
| Dividends | 44,210 | 4,469 |
| Taxes | 5,600 | 6,160 |
| Fixed Asset Increase | 0 | 2,529 |
| | | |
| **Total Expenses** | **$645,060** | **$411,554** |
| | | |
| Total Days | 254 | 254 |
| Hours Per Day | 8 | 8 |
| | | |
| **Total Available Hours** | **2,032** | **2,032** |
| | | |
| **Overhead Rate Per Hour** | **$317.45** | **$202.54** |
| | | |
| **Units Sold** | 12,495 | 7,950 |
| **Price/Unit** | **$51.63** | **$51.77** |

$ ™ Overhead
Rate
**FREE** @
**LesLaMotte.com**

## Services Overheads

| | | | |
|---|---|---|---|
| 1 | Facility Cleaning and Maintence | 26 | Leased Space or Offices |
| 2 | Accountant | 27 | Legal for Incorporation |
| 3 | Advertising | 28 | Lunchroom |
| 4 | Bookshelves | 29 | Marketing |
| 5 | Cell Phones | 30 | Miscellaneous Things |
| 6 | Conference Table & Chairs | 31 | Online services |
| 7 | Cost of Business License(s) | 32 | Overhead Costs |
| 8 | CPA - Certified Public Accountant | 33 | Painting |
| 9 | Decorations | 34 | Parking |
| 10 | Chairs & Desks | 35 | Phones |
| 11 | Electric Hand Tools | 36 | Printer/Copier/Scanner |
| 12 | Electric Saws & Other | 37 | Projector/Large Screen HDV |
| 13 | Electricity | 38 | Purchase Space or Offices |
| 14 | Equipment Lease | 39 | Security |
| 15 | First Aid | 40 | Showroom Displays |
| 16 | Foam Flooring for Warehous | 41 | Showroom Products |
| 17 | Furniture | 42 | Snow Removal |
| 18 | Graphic Design | 43 | Software Licensed/Each Computer |
| 19 | Hand Lift Pallet Truck | 44 | Tables & Chairs |
| 20 | Hand Tools | 45 | Office General Hand Tools |
| 21 | Heat / Cooling | 46 | Visa Card Device(s |
| 22 | High Speed Internet Service | 47 | Walkie Talkies |
| 23 | Instore Displays | 48 | Washable Carpets for Halls |
| 24 | Large Warehouse Stacks | 49 | Website Engine Development |
| 25 | Leased Cars | 50 | Website Updating |
| | | 51 | White or Electronic Note Board |

## Manufacturing Overheads

| | | | |
|---|---|---|---|
| 1 | Overhead Costs | 18 | Online services |
| 2 | Facility Cleaning and Maintence | 19 | Painting |
| 3 | Air Compressor | 20 | Parking |
| 4 | Chairs & Desks | 21 | Printer/Copier/Scanner |
| 5 | Decorations | 22 | Phones |
| 6 | Desks | 23 | Powered Lift Truck |
| 7 | Electric Hand Tools | 24 | Miscellaneous Things |
| 8 | Electric Saws & Other | 25 | Security |
| 9 | Equipment Lease | 26 | Snow Removal |
| 10 | First Aid | 27 | Software Licensed/Each Computer |
| 11 | Foam Flooring for Warehous | 28 | Specialized Machines |
| 12 | Hand Lift Pallet Truck | 29 | Tables 7 Chairs - Lunchroom |
| 13 | Hand Tools | 30 | Tool Air Installation |
| 14 | High Speed Internet Service | 31 | Sepicialized Tools |
| 15 | Large Warehouse Stacks | 32 | Walkie Talkies |
| 16 | Leased Truck or Delivery Vehicle | 33 | WIFI devices |
| 17 | Lunchroom | 34 | Product Jigs |
| 18 | Online services | | |

## Executive Overheads

| | | | |
|---|---|---|---|
| 1 | Facility Cleaning and Maintence | 23 | Legal for Incorporation |
| 2 | Accountant | 24 | Lunchroom |
| 3 | Advertising | 25 | Marketing |
| 4 | Bookshelves | 26 | Online services |
| 5 | Cell Phones | 27 | Painting |
| 6 | Conference Table & Chairs | 28 | Parking |
| 7 | Chairs & Desks | 29 | Printer/Copier/Scanner |
| 8 | Cost of Business License(s) | 30 | Phones |
| 9 | CPA - Certified Public Accountant | 31 | Projector/Large Screen HDV |
| 10 | Decorations | 32 | Miscellaneous Things |
| 11 | Desks | 33 | Security |
| 12 | Equipment Lease | 34 | Showroom Displays |
| 13 | Electricity | 35 | Showroom Products |
| 14 | First Aid | 36 | Software Licensed/Each Compute |
| 15 | Furniture | 37 | Specialized Machines |
| 16 | Graphic Design | 38 | Tables |
| 17 | Hand Tools | 39 | Visa Card Device(s |
| 18 | Heat / Cooling | 40 | Washable Carpets for Halls |
| 19 | High Speed Internet Service | 41 | Website Engine Development |
| 20 | In-store Displays | 42 | Website Updating |
| 21 | Leased Cars | 43 | White or Electronic Note Board |
| 22 | Leased Space or Offices | 44 | WIFI devices |
| | | 45 | Window Treatments |

## Xtra Lite Display Systems Inc — Income Statement

| | 12 Months Ending Dec 31 | | | | 30-Apr | 17-May |
|---|---|---|---|---|---|---|
| | 2000 | 2001 | 2002 | 2003 | 2004 | 2004 |
| Sales | 1,166,857 | 1,100,870 | 1,044,767 | 979,674 | 327,957 | 363,214 |
| Cost of Goods | 622,414 | 485,966 | 415,158 | 369,053 | 133,358 | 152,050 |
| | | | | | | |
| **Gross Profit** | **544,443** | **614,904** | **629,609** | **610,621** | **194,599** | **211,164** |
| | | | | | | |
| Expenses | | | | | | |
| Personnel | 182,603 | 215,940 | 179,482 | 191,037 | 58,240 | 69,588 |
| Building Costs | 41,041 | 82,709 | 92,681 | 87,631 | 30,250 | 30,695 |
| Insurance | 12,237 | 15,740 | 12,673 | 15,988 | 5,146 | 6,443 |
| Promotion | 94,975 | 62,718 | 59,565 | 59,647 | 19,073 | 20,718 |
| Professional Fees | 7,670 | 23,565 | 58,287 | 46,934 | 4,856 | 6,050 |
| Product Development | | 1,861 | 11,397 | 15,785 | 545 | 545 |
| Communication | 21,842 | 25,891 | 41,436 | 25,718 | 7,078 | 8,380 |
| Equipment | 12,142 | 19,229 | 22,691 | 18,737 | 9,209 | 11,103 |
| Fixed Asset Disposal | | | 13,641 | 7,961 | | |
| Section 124 Depr | | | 24,000 | 12,948 | | |
| Depreciation | 53,695 | 57,813 | 33,377 | 24,089 | 7,288 | 9,110 |
| Amortization | 2,610 | 4,352 | 4,834 | 5,110 | 1,616 | 2,020 |
| Professional Development | | 3,008 | | 503 | 494 | 494 |
| Patent Renewal Fees | | | 11,844 | 2,000 | 1,211 | 1,211 |
| Bad Debt | 19,413 | | 3,932 | 1,889 | | |
| Service Charges | 16,064 | 18,492 | 14,316 | 14,191 | 3,744 | 4,851 |
| Miscellaneous | 3,214 | 4,007 | 3,227 | (665) | 300 | 300 |
| **Total Expenses** | **467,506** | **535,325** | **587,383** | **529,503** | **149,050** | **171,508** |
| | | | | | | |
| **Net Operating Income** | **76,937** | **79,579** | **42,226** | **81,118** | **45,549** | **39,656** |
| | | | | | | |
| Other Income | | | | | | |
| Sale of Patents/Trademarks | | | | 5,728 | | |
| Law Suite Proceeds | | | | 20,000 | 10,000 | 10000 |
| **Total Other Income** | | | | **25,728** | **10,000** | **10,000** |
| | | | | | | |
| Other Expense | | | | | | |
| Interest Expense | 6,157 | 15,295 | 12,544 | 22,408 | 4,066 | 4,987 |
| Litigation Costs | | | | 22,703 | | |
| Abandoned Patents | | | | 7,449 | | |
| Abandoned Product Lines | | | | 10,863 | | |
| **Total Other Expenses** | **6,157** | **15,295** | **12,544** | **63,423** | **4,066** | **4,987** |
| | | | | | | |
| **Net Income** | **70,780** | **64,284** | **29,682** | **43,423** | **51,483** | **44,669** |

Note: Depreciation shown here reflects tax depreciation.

## Xtra Lite Display Systems Inc — Balance Sheet

| | As of December 31 | | | | As of | As of |
|---|---|---|---|---|---|---|
| | 2000 | 2001 | 2002 | 2003 | 4/30/04 | 5/17/04 |
| Cash | 8,625 | 10,726 | (21,040) | (14,729) | (3,128) | 28,681 |
| Receivables | 33,226 | 22,795 | 42,350 | 34,368 | 93,723 | 63,475 |
| Inventory | 159,083 | 83,935 | 92,804 | 60,374 | 62,770 | 58,766 |
| Total Current Assets | 200,934 | 117,456 | 114,114 | 80,013 | 153,365 | 150,922 |
| | | | | | | |
| Fixed Assets | 203,819 | 262,002 | 252,370 | 239,912 | 241,424 | 241,424 |
| Accumulated Depr | (115,026) | (169,322) | (172,503) | (191,945) | (199,233) | (201,055) |
| Total Fixed Assets (see Note 1) | 88,793 | 92,680 | 79,867 | 47,967 | 42,191 | 40,369 |
| | | | | | | |
| Other Assets | | | | | | |
| Organization Costs | 155 | 155 | 155 | 155 | 155 | 155 |
| Patent Costs | 57,733 | 71,903 | 72,725 | 69,633 | 69,733 | 69,733 |
| Accumulated Amortization | (1,430) | (9,299) | (15,011) | (16,102) | (17,718) | (18,122) |
| Prepaid Expenses | 8,559 | 10,661 | 10,874 | 15,265 | 11,865 | 11,865 |
| Total Other Assets | 65,017 | 73,420 | 68,743 | 68,951 | 64,035 | 63,631 |
| | | | | | | |
| **Total Assets** | **354,744** | **283,556** | **262,724** | **196,931** | **259,591** | **254,922** |
| | | | | | | |
| Liabilities | | | | | | |
| Accounts Payable | 242,099 | 63,004 | 88,363 | 56,471 | 92,104 | 93,027 |
| | | | | | | |
| Line of Credit | 45,000 | 65,000 | 40,000 | 35,000 | 30,000 | 33,000 |
| Bank Loan | 38,652 | 109,711 | 94,320 | 65,004 | 64,547 | 64,421 |
| Lease | | | 30,299 | 21,680 | 18,517 | 17,703 |
| Total Liabilities | 325,751 | 237,715 | 252,982 | 178,155 | 205,168 | 208,151 |
| | | | | | | |
| Equity | 28,993 | 45,841 | 9,742 | 18,776 | 54,423 | 46,771 |
| | | | | | | |
| **Total Liabilities & Equity** | **354,744** | **283,556** | **262,724** | **196,931** | **259,591** | **254,922** |

Note 1:
The Depreciation reflected on this Balance Sheet is Tax Depreciation.
In addition we have written off approximately $67,000 of obsolete molds, computers and other miscellaneous equipment.

*Wood Chopping Your Business Plan*

Best Advertising agreement we made was to Support Minnesota Business Magazine with our products and receive a full page color ad in their magazine per month and always present at their mini-shows. It's all about "eyeballs" consistently.

| Direct Mail Campaign | | |
| --- | --- | --- |
| Size of Lists | 2,900 | |
| List Rental | 0.15 | each |
| Printing Price | 0.77 | |
| Mailing House Costs | 0.12 | |
| Postage | 0.22 | |
| Sub Total | 1.26 | |
| Total | 3,644.00 | |
| | | Rate of Return |
| Percent of Returns | 36.25 | 1.25% |
| Potiential Sale Price | 500.00 | |
| Potiential Revenue | 18,125.00 | Average Closes |
| Minimum Close Ratio | 25% | 9.06 |
| Revenue Generated | 4,531.25 | |
| Breakeven Cost | 3,644.00 | |
| Net Diff | 887.25 | |

| Card Deck Campaign | | |
| --- | --- | --- |
| Size of Lists | 100,000 | |
| Total Cost | 2,300.00 | |
| Sub Total | 2,300.00 | |
| Total | 0.02 | each |
| | | Rate of Return |
| Percent of Returns | 1,250.00 | 1.25% |
| Potiential Sale Price | 500.00 | |
| Potiential Revenue | 625,000.00 | Average Closes |
| Minimum Close Ratio | 5% | 62.50 |
| Revenue Generated | 31,250.00 | |
| Breakeven Cost | 2,300.00 | |
| Net Diff | 28,950.00 | |

**Xtra Lite Display Systems Inc**
**2006 Goal Sheet**
**YTD ending 4/30/06**

| Date | Goal | Actual | Over (Short) |
|---|---|---|---|
| 4/30/06 | 1.1 | 14.7 | 13.6 |

### YTD Big Picture

| | YTD | # of Days | Daily Production |
|---|---|---|---|
| Annual Goal | 1,183,425 | 251 | 4,715 |
| Actual Income To Date | 409,397 | 84 | 4,874 |
| Over (Short) Goal | (774,028) | 167 | 4,635 |
| % Completed | 34.6% | 33.5% | 3.4% |

### MTD Big Picture

| | MTD | # of Days | Daily Production |
|---|---|---|---|
| April Goal | 78,406 | 20 | 3,920 |
| Actual Income To Date | 144,197 | 20 | 7,210 |
| Over (Short) Goal | 65,791 | 0 | |
| % Completed | 183.9% | 100.0% | 83.9% |

### YTD Displays/Accessories/Misc

| | YTD | # of Days | Daily Production |
|---|---|---|---|
| Annual Goal | 865,960 | 251 | 3,450 |
| Actual Income To Date | 306,756 | 84 | 3,652 |
| Over (Short) Goal | (559,204) | 167 | 3,349 |
| % Completed | 35.4% | 33.5% | 5.9% |

### MTD Displays/Accessories/Misc

| | MTD | # of Days | Daily Production |
|---|---|---|---|
| April Goal | 59,601 | 20 | 2,980 |
| Actual Income To Date | 125,895 | 20 | 6,295 |
| Over (Short) Goal | 66,294 | 0 | |
| % Completed | 211.2% | 100.0% | 111.2% |

### YTD Graphics

| | YTD | # of Days | Daily Production |
|---|---|---|---|
| Annual Goal | 317,465 | 251 | 1,265 |
| Actual Income To Date | 102,641 | 84 | 1,222 |
| Over (Short) Goal | (214,824) | 167 | 1,286 |
| % Completed | 32.3% | 33.5% | -3.4% |

### MTD Graphics

| | MTD | # of Days | Daily Production |
|---|---|---|---|
| April Goal | 18,805 | 20 | 940 |
| Actual Income To Date | 18,302 | 20 | 915 |
| Over (Short) Goal | (503) | 0 | |
| % Completed | 97.3% | 100.0% | -2.7% |

### YTD Goal April 30th Analysis

| | Goal | To Date | Over(Short) |
|---|---|---|---|
| Displays | 244,205 | 306,756 | 62,551 |
| Graphics | 111,181 | 102,641 | (8,540) |
| Total | 355,386 | 409,397 | 54,011 |

To Be On Target As Of April 30th We Must Do: 0

### MTD Goal Analysis

| | MTD Goal | MTD Achieved | Over/(Short) |
|---|---|---|---|
| Displays | 59,601 | 125,895 | 66,294 |
| Graphics | 18,805 | 18,302 | (503) |
| MTD Totals | 78,406 | 144,197 | 65,791 |

To Reach April Goal - This is What We Have Left To Do: 0

### Goal Per Day Til The End Of The Month (YTD Goal)

| | # of Days Remaining | Goal Per Day |
|---|---|---|
| Displays | 0 | |
| Graphics | 0 | |
| Total | | |

### Goal Per Day Til The End Of The Month (Apr Goal Only)

| | # of Days Remaining | Goal Per Day |
|---|---|---|
| Displays | 0 | |
| Graphics | 0 | |
| Total | | |

### TO DATE: THIS YEAR VERSUS LAST YEAR

| | 2006 | 2005 | % of Chg |
|---|---|---|---|
| Displays | 306,756 | 186,544 | 64.4% |
| Graphics | 102,641 | 90,644 | 13.2% |
| Total | 409,397 | 277,188 | 47.7% |
| Cost of Goods Sold | 163,718 | 119,040 | 37.5% |
| Expenses | 167,551 | 176,241 | -4.9% |
| Other Income | | 0 | |
| Other Expenses | | 0 | |
| Net Income | 78,128 | (18,093) | 531.8% |
| Dividends | (15,566) | 12,714 | |
| Net Income After Dividends | 62,562 | (5,379) | |

### MTD: THIS YEAR VERSUS LAST YEAR

| | 2006 | 2005 | % of Chg |
|---|---|---|---|
| Displays | 125,895 | 45,528 | 176.5% |
| Graphics | 18,302 | 15,332 | 19.4% |
| Total | 144,197 | 60,860 | 136.9% |

Goal is based on 11% Growth from Last Yr in Frames & Accessories
Goal is based on 4% Growth from Last Yr in Graphics

### YTD GOAL VS ACTUAL PICTURE

| | |
|---|---|
| YTD March 31st Goal | 276,980 |
| MTD Apr Goal | 78,406 |
| Total Goal To Date | 355,386 |
| YTD Actual | 409,397 |
| Over (Short) of Goal To Date | 54,011 |

## Double Entry Accounting Principles

**Assets = Liabilities + Equities**

| Assets | Liabilities |
|---|---|
| Current | Current |
| Long Term | Long Term |
| | Equity |
| | (Ownership & Stock) |

**Total Assets** = **Total Liabilities**

## Income Statement
(The Moving Picture)

**Revenue**

**– Direct Costs**

**= Gross Profit**

**– General Admin Expenses**
**+ / – Other Income and Expenses**

**= Net Profit**

**Goal Sheet**
FREE @
LesLaMotte.com

# Product Price Analysis

| Product Name | | | | |
|---|---|---|---|---|
| **36x72 XL1 Vert** | | **X1672F** | | |
| **Non-Inventoried Parts** | **Qty** | **Cost Per** | **Cost** | |
| 1 Fit and Finish Labor | 1 | 5.00 | 5.00 | X |
| 2 Shipping In | 1 | 5.00 | 5.00 | X |
| 3 Shipping Out | 1 | 1.33 | 1.33 | |
| 4 Instruction Sheets | 1 | 0.16 | 0.16 | X |
| 5 Labels | | | 0.25 | |
| 6 Poly Bag | 1 | 0.15 | 0.15 | X |
| **Inventoried Parts** | **Qty** | **Cost Per Unit** | **Cost** | |
| 1 PMD13K | 4 | 0.25 | 1.00 | X |
| 2 PMD9S | 2 | 0.10 | 0.20 | X |
| 3 PMD9K | 2 | 0.10 | 0.20 | X |
| 4 PMS875 | 1 | 0.28 | 0.28 | X |
| 5 PMS8V | 1 | 0.19 | 0.19 | X |
| 6 PMS2W | 2 | 0.05 | 0.10 | X |
| 7 PT1336 | 2 | 2.08 | 4.16 | X |
| 8 PT910WO | 3 | 0.44 | 1.32 | X |
| 9 PT926W | 7 | 1.03 | 7.21 | X |
| 10 PT926WO | 2 | 0.91 | 1.82 | X |
| 11 PMS19 | 1 | 0.75 | 0.75 | X |

| | | |
|---|---|---|
| Non-Inventory Items | $ | 10.31 |
| Inventory Items | $ | 17.23 |
| Percent of Increase **5%** | $ | 0.86 |
| **Total Product Cost** | **$** | **28.40** |

**Notes:**

| | | | | |
|---|---|---|---|---|
| | **$28.40** | | **Burden** | **Product** |
| Frames | $50.84 | 79% | $22.44 | X |
| Graphics | $44.31 | 56% | $15.90 | |
| Travel Cases | $37.21 | 31% | $8.80 | |
| Accessories | $39.19 | 38% | $10.79 | |
| Other | $50.84 | 79% | $22.44 | |
| **Total Cost + Burden** | **$50.84** | | | |
| Calculated Net Profit % Goal | 500.00% | | $254.19 | Profit |
| Max. Big Box Discount Rate | 50.00% | | $127.10 | $127.10 |
| **Set Retail Price** | **$254.99** | | 19.94% | **$204.15** |

**Overhead Rate Calculation Per Product**
Based on the Percentage of Difference Between Costs and Revenue

Product Price Analysis FREE @ LesLaMotte.com

| | | | | |
|---|---|---|---|---|
| | **$28.40** | | **Burden** | **Product** |
| Frames | $50.84 | 79% | $22.44 | X |
| Graphics | $44.31 | 56% | $15.90 | |
| Travel Cases | $37.21 | 31% | $8.80 | |
| Accessories | $39.19 | 38% | $10.79 | |
| Other | $50.84 | 79% | $22.44 | |
| **Total Cost + Burden** | **$50.84** | | | |

**Overhead Rate Calculation Per Product**
Based on the Percentage of Difference Between Costs and Revenue

Calculated Net Pr · *fx* · SUMIF ▾ ( H28:H32 ▾ ),"x", ( E28:E32 ▾ ) |

Make a full *Price Analysis Xcel Sheet* for every *Product* you sell. If they are used as universal parts in other *Products* make a separate *Subpart Sheet.* Add the *Price* for each *Product* and *Subpart* so that all costs will be calculated plus your burden for specific areas of income to add the correct business burden to each *Finished Salable Product*. This form will be able to instantly tell you the correct price plus manufacturing and packaging burden if you put in the burden per class of product. The Burden percentage is made based on the classes percentage of the product in your sales category from your accounting. This must be updated monthly, quarterly, and yearly. Visit LesLaMotte.com and download a *Free* Mac Numbers document or build your own program.

# Trademarks & Patents - Two Forms of Legal Defense

**Personal Leather Bound Note Book**
*Invention - Blank*
*Writing - Lined*

**"First Art"**
*Shown to a trusted friend and they, read it tell you they understand it and sign it and establish the date of signing.*

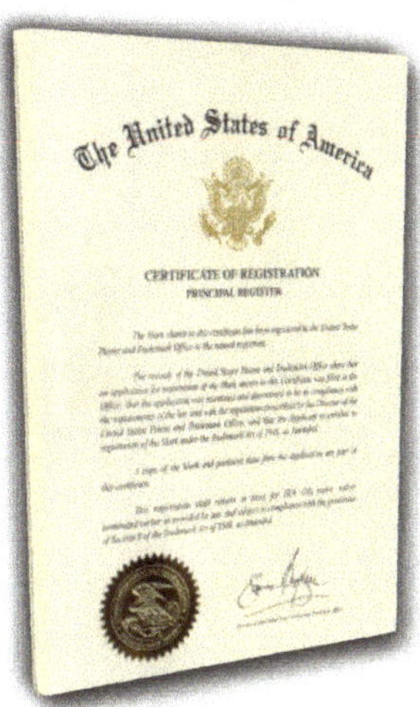

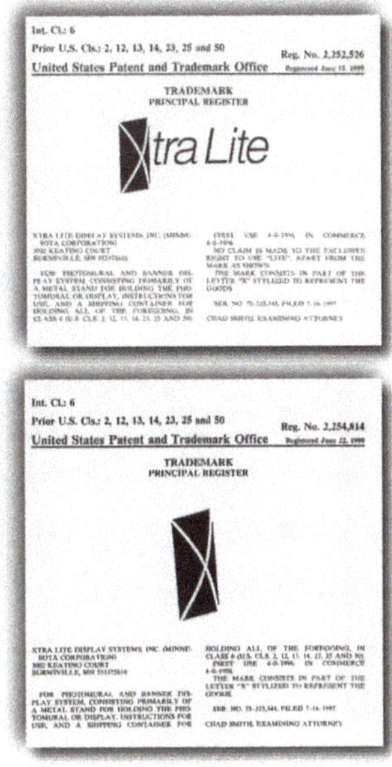

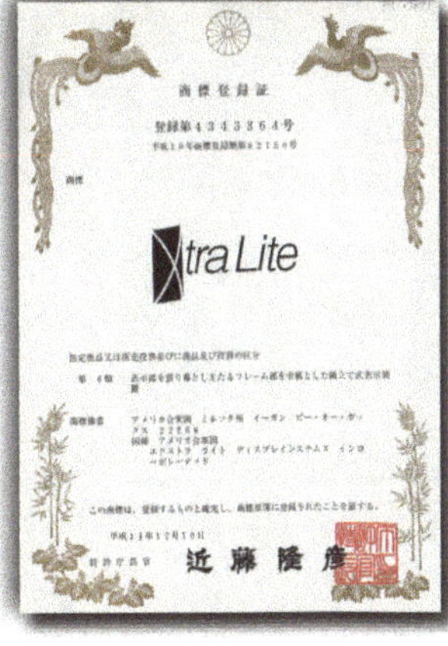

**Xtra Lite Displays®**
Five US Registered Trademarks

- Japanese
- Australia

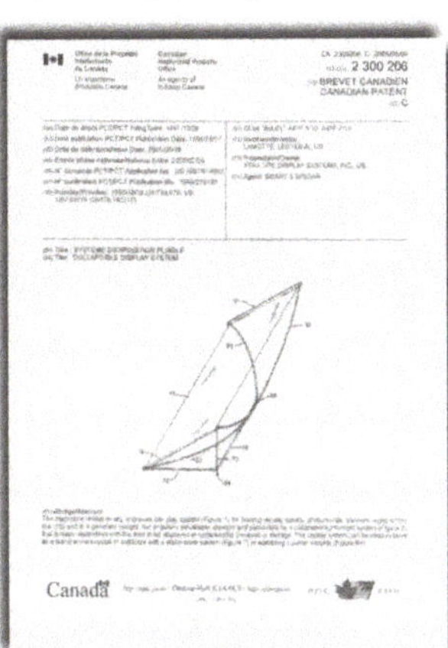

**Xtra Lite Displays®**
Five US Patents &
Three International Patents
- European
- Australian
- Canadian

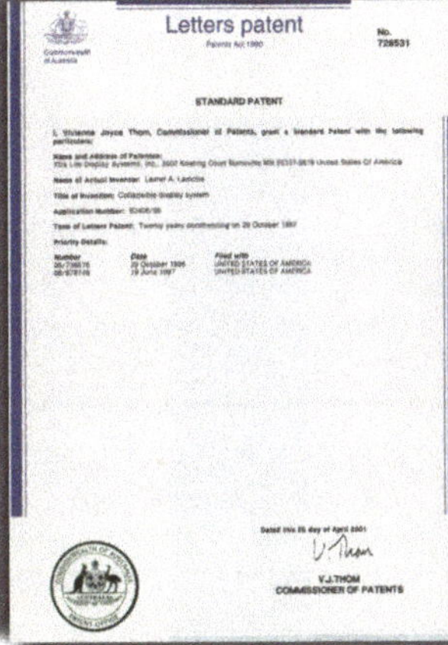

**Over $100,000 Investment**

USPTO.gov

**Xtra Lite Displays®** Burnsville Chamber of Commerce – Open House

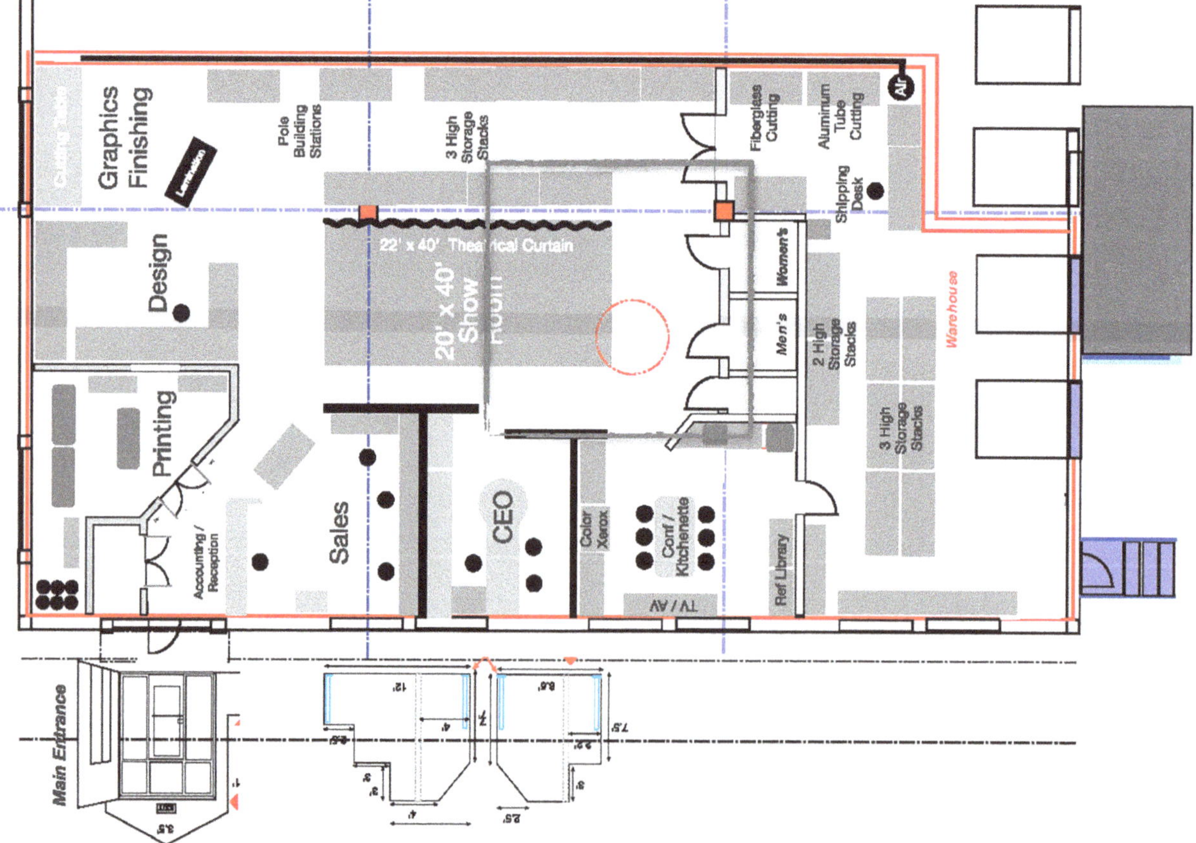

## Preparing Your Passport to the World

### It's Time to Start Your Engines

#### Airports Check-ins and in the Air

Make sure you have a passport that will be legal for at least as long as the expected duration of your stay. As soon as you know you will be traveling, check for the need to apply for a Visa well in advance of your planned departure. The country you are traveling to may require a letter from the company inviting you to be there and stating the reason why and for how long.

Make sure to know the cost of the entry visa so that if you are going to wrap in the costs of the trip into a proposal, you don't forget to input those extra costs that add up quickly. Be aware that some country embassies require that you go in person to apply or be there in person to pay for and receive your passport therefore, it may cost you an additional flight to travel to Chicago or Washington, DC to apply in person.

Go to your local drugstore and get the two passport photos you will need. Then go to your local post office or place in your city that arranges for passports, and make sure you apply for the passport card in addition. This passport card will not get you on a plane; however, if you lose your passport it will get you an immediate temporary replacement. I once lost mine in Germany on my way to Spain while sitting at a bar for a drink. It must have slipped out of my pocket. I panicked for a moment and told the security police there, and then I heard an announcement that someone had found it and it was returned to me. If I had not found it, I would have had to board the plane and then when I arrived in Spain, I would have been forced to buy a new ticket back to the US. So the extra cost of about $125 is well worth it.

If you were to lose your passport by having this additional back up device, you can instantly apply for a new passport and have it available when you reach your new destination or the processing may delay you, but you can get a new one much quicker and easier with that card.

Knowing that in advance will allow you to add that cost to your overall budget or proposal of expenses. This passport card will not give you access to get on the plane, but it can give you instant access to receiving a new passport fast.

## Medical Preparations

Check your country of destination for medical alerts and take any shots required by the country or suggested by your physician at your travel clinic. Make sure you have your medical records up to date and keep them with you as you travel with your visa in case you will be asked while traveling in country or embarking to another one.

## Your Connection, Cabs, Trains, and Planes

You may have to take a short trip by rail, say in England out to the countryside from Heathrow airport, which involves a quick cab to the train station. Traveling to a small village where your host will probably pick you up and bring you to a bed-and-breakfast to stay close by their offices dropping you off and picking you up in the morning for your meetings. Always stay in bed-and-breakfast places in England because they are very cute and quaint. Another benefit is you will meet other travelers and the host family helping you to feel like you are at home with friends at dinner and breakfast.

## Where to Book Hotels in Other Countries

When I was in Germany, I stayed in a local downtown hotel that was very nice, however, costly. I have also stayed in Germany at their heritage hotels down in old town, which is an interesting view of living in a working neighborhood with beautiful paved streets and the classically designed building painted in harmonious colors with cathedrals and small bars and gift shops or local food and fish markets.

Even if you don't drink beer, you must have some of those dark beers while you are in Germany. They go down very smooth, and you imbibe some of the local atmosphere. When I have been at the Messes *(large trade show halls—they are gigantic)* in Düsseldorf, I would take the underground morning train out to the Messe. It was very nice to see the neighborhoods, and it takes you right in front of the doors to the large halls. At night, when you can't walk any longer, you just hop the train back in the evening and get off at your stop, and you can reach most hotels in a few minutes downtown. Just remember in Germany just find the sign for the subway and press the button and an elevator comes up out of the center of the street and takes you down… very interesting and kind of mind bending at first.

While I was in Shanghai, China, I stayed at a very luxurious hotel with all-marble floors with all the luxuries you would expect. Nice rooms with new furniture and TVs

The traffic going anywhere was unbelievable and probably very similar to New York and Los Angeles. The trade shows were held in independent temporary buildings set up in open areas just outside the city, which I am not sure they are there because they were tearing down the old town and building the new one so fast I am not sure I would recognize the city anymore. The trade shows in China are very similar to others I have seen around the world. However, there are literally fifteen to twenty cute little Chinese dolls at every booth who like people at Walmart, that can't tell you anything about the products anyway. Chinese exhibits tend to be all about the hardware, and they don't really sell any services although that may have changed recently.

## Trains

Good if you feel comfortable possibly having to read other languages to get to the right loading zones and into the correct lines to purchase the tickets, and finding the location to get on the train. After that, it is all about how to know if you are at the right location because there's none of the normal English or same shape and colored signs you are used to and then there is the all important language barrier, however, almost everywhere in the world you can find someone who speaks English to help you when you reach out for their help. Most large cities today have both their language and English on most of the signs in travel zones. In Europe, however, because most of the people speak up to five other languages and grow up using them, you may not find consistent English signing, so making a quick friend is always the best policy. If you are going to places like Italy from Germany, don't take a plane— just hop on the train and explore the Alps as you travel through some of the most beautiful mountains in the world in comfort.

## Rental Cars

If you are going to try to drive in a foreign country, you need to obtain an International Driver's License ($50–$100) good in any country outside of the US from your local AAA office or Driver's license bureau. The largest challenge in the *"wrong sided or left"* orientated road countries is the quick reorientation of your automatic car checking response. You must learn it quickly or get nailed at the first crosswalk. Take sometime and figure it out, I know it is very hard to do and it may take a while. I have driven in England and Scotland with my friend Peter who went to school there, so he could easily switch back and forth.

Your immediate weakness shows up from your automatic car's subconscious sense of safety checking is totally off, and you run the risk of a possible easy accident by just not being ready to look in the right direction on the right side at the right time. Believe me, I even had a hard time walking across the street because the oncoming traffic is totally located in an opposite direction than you are used to, leaving you possibly extremely exposed to surprises and frequent honks.

If your travel a lot it may be worth the money spent to buy a pre-check-in card. The cost is about $125. The card gives you access to checking in at the non or low-impact check locations. If you are a senior citizen, you could possibly get this without paying the extra money at the check-in based on being over sixty-five.

## *How to Prepare Yourself Before and While You're In-fight for Quick Recovery upon Arrival*

When you embark on an extremely long distances flight such as to China and India, don't try to get the cheapest flight as cheap don't mean much when your back and legs are dying in a cramped airline seat for twenty-two hours. I have often taken a standard seat location for the long trip from Minneapolis to Tokyo, but for the trip from Tokyo to South Korea or Shanghai, China, I would purchase a first-class seat. There are two reasons. Once you arrive at the first destination, you are getting very tired. The cattle seats at the back of the bus are not very comfortable, especially as you get closer to your destination where many local or country people will come on and speak other languages, have tons of extra luggage because they are returning home. So give yourself a break and take the last leg of the journey in style and arrive rested, well fed, and well taken care of. Possibly even get some extra shut eye before you arrive at your destination. Take it from me; the slight cost increase is well worth it compared to first class for the entire trip. Afford yourself some tenderness, after all, you are flying which at times is quite stressful in itself.

While on the plane in long flights, drink water with fresh squeezed lemon or Sprite as the lemon helps to detoxify your brain and keeps you hydrated and from getting stuffed up feeling. The air-conditioning on planes are notorious for sucking the life out of you before you realize it. Eat something good so you feel relaxed. Try to give yourself some shut-eye, even a short nap, to help bring back your strength. After your short nap, try to get up and walk around the cabin. If it is one of the new Airbuses, then you have a complete track to walk down one side to the rear, stop at the rest room, then walk back. This will keep your blood flowing and save you from cramping up. If you do occasionally get leg cramps easily, bring along anti-leg cramping pills in a small pill container to make it much easier to relieve the symptoms fast. Also, if you suffer with water retention in your ankles, make sure you absolutely move around or you can run the risk of a stroke.

If you are a man with a beard, it is amazing how fast your whiskers will grow sitting in a plane. For men, bring a small battery-operated shaver. I recommend the one I use is a Braun wet use $15 online and bring it out about an hour before you land. Make sure you have two extra AA batteries in your travel case on the plane. I know it will make you feel much better and relaxed. You can also get up and go to the restroom, put a little liquid hand soap on your face before you shave to lubricate your face for a smooth shave. A better alternative is a small bottle of Shave Secret or sealed straw of shave prep is a welcomed item. To roll your own just clamp off the end of a plastic straw with a bull clamp or plier and place it on the opposite side of the cut you want to seal. Using a barbecue fire starter or lighter while squeezing the end with the pliers, paper clip, or bull clamp put a flame to it melting the plastic and sealing it. Add your fluid, honey, pills, and again just seal it and cut it to at your desired length and seal the edge once more. Caution, if you put in the tube something that contains alcohol, be careful that you don't set it all aflame while sealing. When choosing your shaving fluid, just make sure the fragrance is not overwhelming as planes are very small, and the odor can be a problem for others around you. Now get ready when and if they bring you hot towels (that's the sign of a real classy airlines)—pretty standard on all overseas flights. This will wake you up and make you feel squeaky clean and refreshed, ready to get going to battle or socialize with your business partners immediately when you land.

After eight to twenty-two hours in the air, make sure you bring the little packets of mini toothbrushes that have the small dab of peppermint or cinnamon toothpaste inside the small brush—I like them both—and put them in your purse or travel bag. After you have something to eat, use this small toothbrush to clean and sanitize your teeth. Rinse with your glass of water or liquid, and it will make you feel great and rescue your reputation from those around you by removing that pasty-mouth feeling from the constant drying-out sensation on the flight.

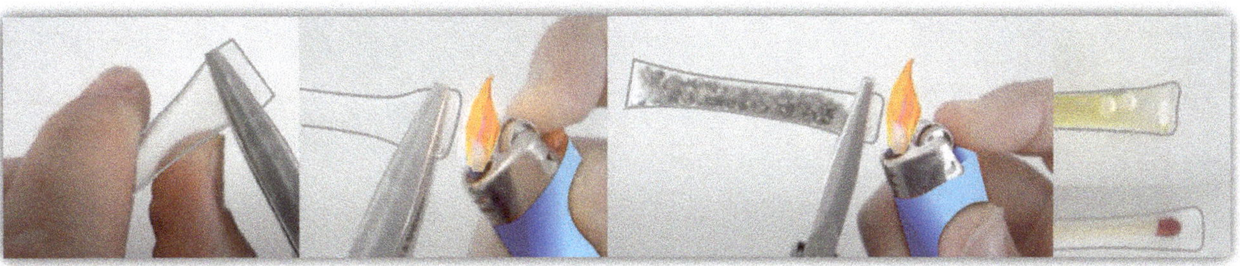



20

I also like to carry some small tooth floss picks, to make sure you don't have to sit for hours with things in your teeth that causes frustration. The spearmint has always been my favorite and a nice fresh touch.

Another small package I always carry on the plain is some kind of gum; I like cinnamon. You can use it for takeoffs and landings. The chewing action helps to keep your ears free from any pressure buildup and depressurize your ears so you can hear again.

Finally, when you get off the plane, hear me out… it is the time of the place you land. Just force yourself to recalibrate your internal time clock to the time there. Don't get hung up on this is the time for me at home is—just forget about even talking about that. I guarantee it won't help, and it will slow you down from attending to your business. To make up for your lack of sleep, just try to take a few cat naps when you can or go get a cup of coffee to give you the strength and comfort to continue being in the right zone. It is always a good idea to go out and have something to eat as soon as you can to help give you a feeling of renewed energy. Go to bed early and hope for a good night sleep, and get ready for the activities of the next day. When I can't get to sleep and I am in a bed-and-breakfast or hotel, I always ask for a small glass of wine or warm milk and that usually calms me down and allows me to float off easier.

Happy flying and make sure you get to know the person next to you. Who knows, they could be your next customer or someone to tell you about your next ***Imagineering idea… Happy exploring!***

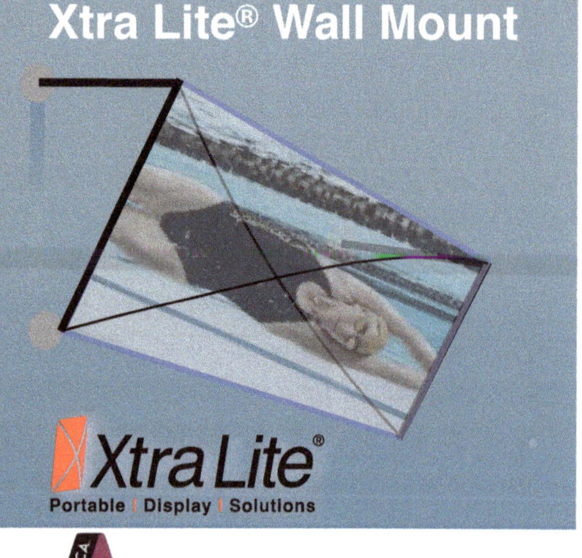


Xtra Lite® Wall Mount at the Speedo Store in the Mall of America.

# AIR FLIGHT PRE-FLIGHT CHECK LIST – PAGE 1

Pre-Flight Check List FREE @ LesLaMotte.com

**20**



| | Item | Task |
|---|---|---|
| 1 | ☐ **Letter of Invitation?** | From company you want to visit in restricted countries i.e. China. |
| 2 | ☐ **Visa** | Make sure you consider whether you have to travel to purchase it. |
| 3 | ☐ **Passport Application** | Go to your government building or the post office. |
| 4 | ☐ **Passport Photo** | They usually provide you with 2 for $10-$25 |
| 5 | ☐ **Passport Card** | Buy with Passport approximately $100-$125. |
| 6 | ☐ **Travel Clinic** | Go to your local Travel Clinic to received any shots required for area. |
| 7 | ☐ **Make Local Travel** | Make sure you are aware of the kinds of ground transportation and price. |
| 8 | ☐ **Exchange Money** | Exchange enough for cash needed in local money for minor expenses on the way out of the airport. |
| 9 | ☐ **Cell Phone** | Make sure you check with your Cell phone company to open International use. Or buy a cheap flip phone and a SIM chip while you are there. |
| 10 | ☐ **Cell Phone 2 SIMs** | If you are going to places like Africa, consider buying a 2nd local SIM card like iPhone's offers in the latest versions. This will allow you to purchase a local card to reduce your costs and still use all of your cell phone apps and numbers. |
| 11 | ☐ **Language** | Possibly prepare by sharpening your knowledge of local languages. |
| 12 | ☐ **International Car or Truck License** | Pick up an international car or truck license in the US approximately $50-$100 for 3-5 years. |
| 13 | ☐ **Check Insurance?** | Make sure you understand your Insurance coverage and international limitations. |
| 14 | ☐ **Prepare for Driving Road Sides** | Make sure that you realize that driving sides of the road change in every country. Get some help if you plan to begin driving Left sided driving. |

# AIR FLIGHT PRE-FLIGHT CHECK LIST – PAGE 2

**20**



| | Item | Task |
|---|---|---|
| 15 | ☐ **Pre-Check-in Card** | If you want to pre-board without going through long lines you can purchase a Fast Pass Card. Approximately $100-$300 approximately 2 weeks to a month before. |
| 16 | ☐ **Consider First Class** | Consider First Class as a last leg of long trips to avoid the local traffic, local people, and customs of foreign countries as they typical carry more on-board luggage. |
| 17 | ☐ **Hydrate Before Flights** | Drink enough water as you can before you fly as the plane dehydrates you quickly and you are more susceptible to viruses and decease with a dry mouth and nose. |
| 18 | ☐ **Use Lemon Water** | Using lemon and honey with your water will help to keep your brain from toxification which causes headaches and mental fog and jet lag. |
| 19 | ☐ **Gum** | Bring some gum with as it helps to keep your ears from plugging up as you take off and land. |
| 20 | ☐ **Keep Active** | Stretch and walk around the plane whenever possible. |
| 21 | ☐ **Eat Good Food** | Food will keep your energy up and help to overcome the energy and water losses while inflight. |
| 22 | ☐ **Take Short Naps** | Try to sleep if you can. Consider a light drink or a knockout pill if it will help you sleep. If you can get some warm milk it is a sure thing to put you to sleep like a baby. |
| 23 | ☐ **Have a Beard** | Try to shave with a small battery operated razor an hour before landing. I recommend Mobile Shave (water proof) by Braun. |
| 24 | ☐ **Throw Away Tooth Brush** | Bring a few throw away tooth brushes I use Colgate (micro brushes with Tooth Paste) before landing. |
| 25 | ☐ **Assume the Time** | Assume the time it is where you land and continue on the New time not the one you came from… this will help you quickly adapt to the new time zone. Get a good meal ASAP that gives you some initial additional energy. |
| 26 | ☐ **Take Your PassPort, Tickets, and Medical** | Double check the location of your Ticket(s), Passport(s), Medical paper(s) and Medicine(s) before leaving home or your office. |

# Spread Your Wings

*Poem by Les LaMotte*
*for his son Joshua*

Spread your wings my son,
skyward everyday of your life my son,
set your course high above my son,
not looking back my son,
but to the open sky my son.

For its spring my son,
your wings are strong and steady to take
flight my son, over worlds uncharted, over highest
mountains my son, and roar through deepest
valleys my son.

Take loft in summer currents my son,
spread them wide and far my son,
reach to catch a falling sparrow my son,
dive deep to snatch your prey from troubled waters my son,
stay strong to weather the gales of fall my son.

Build your nest secure my son,
on the highest peaks my son,
breathe the very breath of God my son,
warm and feed your chicks with new life my son.

As winter winds blow cold and your wings wax weak and frail,
watch over them through the cold cold night my son,
spread their wings once again my son,
encourage them in flight my son.

I've spread my wings my son,
Stilled the angry gale with in, my son
wing your way homeward my son,
He's waiting here for you my son.

I'll see you once again my son,
with wings spread wide my son,
with tears of joy my son,
Welcome home my son.

Be at peace my son.





*Preparing Your Passport to the World*